环球卓越
www.geedu.com
谭松柏 / 丛书主编
谭松柏 / 本书主编 李 伦 / 本书副主编

4周攻克雅思听力周计划

英语周计划系列丛书
ENGLISH WEEKLY PLAN SERIES

机械工业出版社
CHINA MACHINE PRESS

"英语周计划系列丛书"是针对我国读者的英语学习特点开发的、以"周"为谋篇布局单位、以"日"为具体实施单元的极具特色的英语辅导用书，具有思维创新、规划科学、目标明确、讲练结合、直击实战等特点。《4周攻克雅思听力周计划》是本系列针对IELTS的一个分册。

编者从雅思听力部分的题型特点和设题规律出发，针对考生复习中经常遇到的问题，为考生提供了一个完整的IELTS听力4周复习方案，每周安排7天（星期一至星期日），合计28天。第一周为您提供雅思听力的基本功训练；第二周是题型渗透策略；第三周针对常考场景进行精练，最后一周设置了7套模拟试题，检验复习成果。4周的安排，目标明确，科学合理，帮助考生理清复习思路，获得理想的考试成绩。

图书在版编目（CIP）数据

4周攻克雅思听力周计划/谭松柏主编.
—北京：机械工业出版社，2011.6（2012.1重印）
（英语周计划系列丛书/谭松柏丛书主编）
ISBN 978-7-111-35008-8

Ⅰ.①4… Ⅱ.①谭… Ⅲ.①IELTS—听说教学—自学参考资料
Ⅳ.①H319.9

中国版本图书馆CIP数据核字（2011）第109365号

机械工业出版社（北京市百万庄大街22号 邮政编码100037）
责任编辑：孙铁军 版式设计：墨格文慧
责任印制：李 妍
北京振兴源印务有限公司印刷
2012年1月第1版第2次印刷
184mm×260mm · 13.75印张 · 350千字
6001—9000册
标准书号：ISBN 978-7-111-35008-8
ISBN 978-7-89433-009-3（光盘）
定价：39.80元（含1CD）

凡购本书，如有缺页、倒页、脱页，由本社发行部调换
电话服务
社服务中心：（010）88361066
销售一部：（010）68326294
销售二部：（010）88379649
读者购书热线：（010）88379203
网络服务
门户网：http://www.cmpbook.com
教材网：http://www.cmpedu.com

丛 书 序

现如今的中国人，上学不再满足于清华、北大，工作也不仅放眼于国企。而是走向一个更为宽广的世界——出国深造和就业。这是中国政治、经济、文化发展的结果，是好事，利国利民，利己利人。然而并非每个有出国梦想的人都能如愿以偿，很多人都被雅思这个拦路虎拦在了国门以内。

由于雅思考核学生听说读写的综合运用能力，这与中国传统的英语教学完全不接轨。尽管近年来中国的外语教学有了很大的改进和发展，但苦于没有语言环境，教学和学习效果依然不理想。加之教育改革周期长，效果缓慢，很多中国考生依然是传统应试教育的产物或二代产物。仔细想来，题做了不少，词汇记了无数，语法也学了很多，但一旦落实到应用，尤其是听说和写作，就最多只能是中式英语，这不符合雅思的考核标准。因此，很多中国考生都万事俱备，只欠雅思，但这雅思一分难求，所以很多考生只能望分兴叹。虽心有不甘，但也只能脚踏实地走进英语课堂，走遍各个培训学校，听遍所有名师课堂。虽感觉老师们说的很有道理，感觉找到了救命稻草，但是，回到家中，冷静下来，却发现自己依然不会说英语，也听不懂，单词记不住，好不容易记住的那些，可能又忘了。

殊不知，语言学习是技能学习，和学开车、学游泳是一个道理。那就是，要想学好外语，必须增加练习，光听“教练”讲道理是不够的。考生在听完名师讲解雅思考试规律和复习技巧以后，还要坐下来，安静地看看书，从中获取养分，夯实英语基本功才是硬道理。不能抱着侥幸心理，想着混过雅思。考生更应该借雅思这个东风，真正把英语水平提高，毕竟，走出国门后，就得靠英语生存、学习和工作了，那时多少分不再是硬道理。

英语的学习必须是听说读写词汇并进，很多考生屡考不过是因为缺乏严密的计划。而且，三天打鱼两天晒网，语言的学习在没有形成能力之前，往往一日不练十日空。因此，要想学好外语，还要作好科学的规划，并按这个规划去执行。很多考生要么完全不知道怎么学习，要么是盲从别人的方法，或是众说纷纭，不知所从。

“英语周计划系列丛书”是在分析考生的现状和种种困难的基础上形成的一整套完善的雅思复习计划。本系列书以提高考生英语应试水平、迅速提高雅思分数为目的，一举两得。雅思周计划共 5 本书，囊括了听、说、读、写四大雅思考试板块，并涵盖学习英语的基本功：词汇。这 5 本书依次是：**《4 周攻克雅思听力周计划》**、**《4 周攻克雅思口语周计划》**、**《4 周攻克雅思阅读周计划》**、**《4 周攻克雅思写作周计划》**、**《4 周攻克雅思词汇周计划》**。

之所以叫周计划，是因为每本书都是以周为单位进行学习。其实，攻克雅思并非有多难，难就难在没有掌握技巧和方法，而本套丛书通过 4 周完整缜密的规划，将听、说、读、写并进，再辅以词汇，引领考生攻克雅思考试大关！

本系列丛书特点如下：

- **系统全面，涵盖雅思考试听说读写四大板块**。让雅思考试备考一气呵成，自成体系。
- **计划科学、完整、缜密，可操作性强**。每本书按 4 周进行，每周 7 天，每天任务具体、清晰、充实。考生无须再去苦恼该干什么，不该干什么。

● **科学的应试备考过程，从易到难，循序渐进**。每本书的第一周是“引进门”，并对雅思考试技能迅速了解；第二周是“打基础”，让考生基本功得到迅速夯实；第三周则是“技巧强化”，迅速提升语言水平，为考试作好充足的准备；而第四周则是“模拟考场”。让考生每天如战马驰骋，实战沙场，以达到考前最佳状态。

● **一书在手，众生皆宜**。这是本丛书的又一大特色。无论是从未涉足雅思考试的新手，还是久经沙场的“考鸭”，本丛书均能满足需求，尤其是对于那些急于攻克雅思考试并渴求获取雅思高分的考生，本丛书更是书海中的首选！

每每在讲课之余，我都能碰到心急如焚的考生；每当看到他们那种求助的眼神，我都暗下决心要为他们做点什么。我也曾是一名外语学习者，也有过和他们一样的困惑和迷茫，但如今，我已是一名从事外语教学多年的老师，责任和使命感促使我必须拿出切实的行动。在全国著名的培训机构——**环球卓越**的大力组织下，一批和我一样热心于雅思教学的师资团队走到了一起，用我们多年的教学成果，共同铸就了我们这套丛书——雅思周计划系列！

路，总是在延伸，一望无尽；但是，路，却有畅通无阻，也有曲折迂回。真心希望，这套周计划能让众多雅思考生少一点犹豫，少一点徘徊，少一点弯路，尽量把大好的青春年华用在有用的事情上。更希望众多的雅思考生，能够成为一名有志的中国学子，早日走出去，在实现自己梦想的同时，也为祖国富强添砖加瓦。我这区区外语教师，也算是不枉十年寒窗了。

谭松柏

2011年元旦于北京

前　言

听说读写听为首，但为何听力总是中国雅思考生的痛？

制约考生听力有三大因素：心理素质不过硬、背景知识不充足、语言基本功不扎实，直接导致的后果是，很多考生虽备战一场但进入考场后却如履薄冰，功亏一篑。

那么，有没有真正实用的方法去攻克和解决这一难题？答案是——有！

作为从事雅思辅导多年的编者，亲眼目睹了太多考生的辛酸和艰难，在此，谨以此书敬献给众多考生，希望能帮大家拨云见雾，助考生一臂之力！

编者结合了考生常遇到的问题，在总结听力题型特点及命题规律的基础上，为考生提供了一个循序渐进、日日有提升、周周有飞跃的4周全面攻克雅思听力的方案，具体说来：

第一周：雅思听力基本功训练。英语听力非一日之功，且受制于读、写、说及词汇和语法等基本技能。针对这一点，周计划的第一周就专练基本功，将听力所需各项基础知识进行提炼，正所谓"高楼不怕地基深"，扎实的基本功才是制胜的关键。

第二周：题型渗透策略。雅思考试涉及不同题型，而如何分门别类攻克是关键。本周结合雅思考试命题规律，将雅思听力出现的题型分类整理到第二周的每一天，逐个题型渗透，直至全部攻克。

第三周：雅思听力常考场景精练。雅思考核考生是否具备出国生存、学习或工作的能力因此，雅思考试往往不是纯语言的考试，而是考核语言出现的各个相关背景知识。本周则将雅思常考场景进行分类布局，让考生如身临其境，直奔主题。

第四周：模拟实战。在前三周循序渐进的基础上，配置以仿真模拟，强化冲刺，真正达到学以致用和迅速提升的目标，快速进入实战状态。

另外，本书将讲与练进行了有机结合。可以说，听力是一日不练十日生的，而如何有序练习，恰如其分地把握好所学知识，这是周计划的优势所在，也是本书一大特色。全书通过4周的安排，目标明确，规划合理，备考精准，是一本完美攻克雅思听力的辅导良书。

参加本书编写的还有詹圣麒、詹景祺、David Speary、刘敏、郭肇焱、谭淑静、李兰荣、许少雄、尹航、石茜、修苗苗、张玲、陈阳、潘秀英、刘晓蓉、李德标、何光锋、梁莉娟、孟宪华，在此表示衷心感谢！

希望本书能成为您备考路上的好伴侣！

编　者

2011年7月于北京

目　　录

4周攻克

雅思听力周计划

第一周　雅思听力基本功训练

本周的学习任务是雅思听力基本功的训练，主要包括了解雅思听力、语音基本功训练，以及微技能训练。

第一周	每日学习内容
星期一	学习、理解英语听力学习的难点和解决方案 了解雅思听力考试流程
星期二	语音基本功练习
星期三	练习听数字，包括：序数词，电话号码，邮政编码，产品编号，时间，年月日，钱的数量表达
星期四	练习听人、地名及字母拼写
星期五	听写练习：听单词、词组、句子、段落
星期六	听对话
星期日	听新闻

星期一

了解雅思听力

今天，我们的主要任务是学习、理解英语听力学习的难点和解决方案；了解雅思听力考试流程。

雅思听力考什么？

1. 雅思听力十大难点

听力位列听说读写之首，可见其重要性。听力往往是中国考生雅思考试的致命弱点，也是出国生存的最大困难之一。听力难具体体现为：

1）The more you want to listen, the more difficult you feel it is（越想听，越是听不懂）；

2）You feel very difficult to concentrate on listening（听力过程中不能集中注意力）；

3）I can catch the first several sentences, but miss the rest information（能听懂前几句话，但余下信息都没听到）；

4）I can catch nearly every word, but fail to get the main idea of the materials（几乎能听懂每一个单词，但是不明白文章大意）；

5）I can not listen with background noise, even a little（在有背景音的情况下，我听不懂/见）；

6）If there is a new word or sentence, I will think about it, then I miss the rest information（听力中碰到生词或新的句型，我需要思考一下，于是后面的信息就错过了）；

7）I can not take notes while listening（不能在听的过程中做笔记）；

8）Sometimes I felt that I was very familiar with the vocabulary, but need time to think about the meaning of them（有时候感觉听力中的部分词汇似曾相识，但需要时间思考才能想出其含义）；

9）I do not have problems in listening, but often fail to fill the blanks（能听懂，但不会做题）；

10）I have no problems in the first two sections, but feel difficult to do the last two sections（听社会性话题没什么困难，但是听不懂学术性话题的听力）。

2. 雅思听力难的三大理由

出现以上听力困难的原因主要有三个。一是心理因素；二是背景知识不足；三是语言基本功不扎实。

很多考生平时练习听力的时候感觉还不错，但一上考场大脑就一片空白，或者是越努力集中注意力听，越是听不懂。其实，是因为太紧张导致的。听力考试发挥最好的时候往往是在考生最为放松的状态下，只有放松的时候才能自信，才能放眼全局，不至于顾此失彼。当然，考试的时候，听力只放一遍，因此，不能紧张，但还是要有紧迫感，这样方能把自己的最佳潜能激发出来，达到最佳考试效果。

雅思考试虽然是考语言水平，但报名参加考试的学生几乎都是以出国留学或移民为目的的。简单地说，雅思要考核考生是否具备出国生存、学习或工作的能力。因此，雅思听力往往不是纯语言的考试，与语言同时出现的是相关背景知识。比如，考生出国必然要租房。因此，租房的场景是雅思听力的常考话题。但如果考生从来没有过租房经历，或对租房知识和相关词汇严重不足，考试的时候自然就非常被动。又如，研究课题的讨论和论文写作的相关内容也经常在雅思听力中出现，但很多考生在中国学习期间没有学习任何相关知识，即便是用母语表达出来，也有听不明白的时候，更不用说是用英语表述出来了。总之，文化、背景知识的储备也是攻克雅思听力必不可少的。

听力往往是语言学习最后被攻克的一项技能。因为听力受制于读、写、说以及词汇、语法和语音。也就是说，如果考生其他技能不好，听力也不可能好，甚至有的考生是其他技能还不错，听力也觉得困难。因为听力，除了以必要的语音、语法、词汇知识为基础外，还要有较强的口语、阅读甚至是写作水平为支撑，并需要一定量的听力训练。因此，要想突破听力，不能仅从听力着手，必须结合各项知识和技能齐头并进，效果方能最佳。

3. 听力与其他技能和知识的紧密关系

- **口语**：听说永远不分家，有听就一定有说；
- **阅读**：阅读能帮考生获取较强的预感，而语感是实现被动听力主动化的主要因素，因为，根据语感，考生往往能在听到一句话的前一半的时候，预知下半句话的意识，或者说话倾向；
- **写作**：写作中能用的语言往往才是考生真正具备的语言，只有达到这个程度，听力的时候才能游刃有余；
- **语音**：如果考生自己的发音不准，听到准确的发音反倒不能迅速辨别了；
- **语法**：听力中对句法的把握会严重影响听力的质量，在誊写听力答案到答题卡上的时候，必须确保语法的准确性；
- **词汇**：词汇永远是越多越好，对听力而言，必须保证词汇掌握得非常熟练，要在听到的时候，不需要任何思索就可以反应过来。

雅思听力该怎么练？

常言道，Practice makes perfect（熟能生巧）。听力尤其需要大量练习。但是也不是说只要大量听就行。听力需要有策略地进行练习，方能事半功倍。

首先，听力练习必须是精听和泛听结合。用精听的方式练习各种听力微技能，但还要通过大量的泛听，以便多次体验不同语言场景和内化各种听力技能，形成能力。精听可以是精听教材，但泛听可以是任何听力材料，可以是英语电视节目，也可以是英语广播，甚至是英语电影、电视剧和歌曲。

听力练习的一个大忌是三天打鱼，两天晒网。英语听力在没有形成能力之前，容易出现一日不练十日空的情况。很多考生经常纳闷，本来练习了一天的听力，感觉很好了，结果第二天或第三天感觉又没了。因此，听力的练习必须要有持续性，最好每天都有，但不必要每天太久。因为，听力练习容易疲倦，而疲倦之后再练习，效果就不明显了，最好每天练习 30 到 40 分钟，也就是雅思考试的时间。这样也容易形成考试状态。

雅思听力的高分往往是听力基本功和考试策略的最佳结合。也就是说在苦练听力基本功的同时，也要不断练习听力考试策略。保证考出与听力水平相吻合或者高于自己听力水平的分数。比如，听力考试中很多答案是可以在听前预测的，或者是可以将填空题预测为更为简单的选择题。

雅思听力考试简介

雅思听力考试时间为 40 分钟，题目分四个部分。每部分 10 题，每题 1 分。第一个部分是日常生活中会发生的对话（通常为二人），第二个部分是生活相关的独白；第三个部分是学术性的对话（通常二人以上），第四个部分为学术论文演讲。四个部分的难度依次增加。通常前三个部分都会分成两段提问，分别回答不同的问题。考生在听完每段录音后会有一小段时间复查，但因为不会重复，所以要求考生即时写出答案。全部录音放完需时 30 分钟，剩余 10 分钟供考生将答案从试卷填写到答题卡上。

The table below provides a summary of IELTS Listening.

Section	Topic Area	Input	Main Skill Focus	Number of Questions
1	Social needs	Conversation with a transactional purpose e.g. finding out about travel services	Listening for and noting specific factual information	10
2	Social needs	Monologue or prompted monologue with a transactional purpose e.g. giving information about a public event	Listening for and noting specific factual information	10
3	Education and training	Discussion between 2 – 4 people in an academic context, e.g. tutorial or seminar	Following a conversation which involves negotiation of meaning. Listening for specific information, attitudes, and speakers' opinions	10
4	Education and training	Monologue in an academic context e.g. lecture	Following an academic argument. Listening for main ideas, specific information, attitude and speaker's opinion	10

听力考试总共四段语音，其中前二段内容以一般生活及社会状态、人际关系不同情况模拟为主，后二段则多围绕教育性、学术性、世界性的主题来探讨。第一、三段以对答为主，二、四段以叙述为主。

在四部分的听力过程中，学生要求答的题目类型非常多，主要有选择题（一般是三选一，也有可能是五选二）；配对题；填图题；填空题；完成句子或是简答题等。这些题都要求考生只能用字母、数字或三个以内的单词作答，答案超过要求数量无效。

在随后的周计划中，我们会按照题型、场景依次展开。

星期二

语音基本功练习

在雅思听力中，很多考生有辨音困难。比如将 390 听成 319，将 20A 听成 28 等。这些都是因为辨音练习不够。然而要想听出语音的差别，首先要求自己发音准确。如果考生自己发音都不准确，那么在听到准确发音的时候，也很难识别，因此，在练习听力辨音之前，首先要自己练习发音。但是，要想练得准确、地道的发音却不是一件易事。学习发音需要反复模仿，而且要一遍一遍地练习。

语音语调的准确地道，首先要求对每个英语的音素发音准确，即要发准每个音标。英语中有 48 个音标。其中元音 20 个，半元音 2 个，辅音 26 个。如下表所示：

Vowels

/ɑː/	/ʌ/	/æ/	/e/	/ɪ/	/iː/
/əː/	/ə/	/ɔː/	/ɔ/	/uː/	/u/
/ei/	/ɑi/	/iə/	/ɔi/		
/uə/	/eə/	/əu/	/ɑu/		

Consonants

/p/	/t/	/k/	/s/	/f/	/θ/	/ʃ/
/b/	/d/	/g/	/z/	/v/	/ð/	/ʒ/
/tʃ/	/tr/	/ts/			/l/	/m/
/dʒ/	/dr/	/dz/			/r/	/n/
					/h/	/ŋ/
	/w/	/j/				

中国考生常犯的语音错误

- /th/ 组合发音不准，常常将其浊音/ð/与/z/，/dz/混淆，或将其清辅音/θ/与/s/混淆。
- 单词末尾的/m/不能发出双唇音，name 读成/nei/。
- 唇齿音/f/和/v/需要上齿咬住下唇再发音，但很多考生与/w/混淆，将 very 读作/weri/。
- 部分地区的考生不能区分/n/和/l/，于是 night 与 light 发音混淆。

试试你的语音基本功

要想听出说话人的发音，必须先确保自己能发音准确，因此，考生需要进行下面的基本功练习：

音　标	例　词
1.[a:]	half，calm，car，farm，dark
2.[ʌ]	love, but, lucky, cut
3.[æ]	bad, land, bank, stamp
4.[e]	bed, desk, head, met

（续）

音　标	例　词
5.[i]	sit, build, miss, myth
6.[i:]	sea, he, see, piece, ceiling
7.[ə:]	bird, girl, serve, nurse
8.[ə]	polite, dollar, doctor, famous
9.[ɔ:]	door, more, sport, ball
10.[ɔ]	hot, want, because
11.[u:]	who, blue, soup, glue
12.[u]	look, put, women,
13.[ei]	cake, bake, lake, fake
14.[ai]	fly, bike, kite, cry
15.[iə]	ear, tear, sneer, beer
16.[ɔi]	boy, toy, toilet, oil
17.[uə]	tour, poor
18.[eə]	pear, air, glare, fair
19.[əu]	bow, know, coat, own
20.[au]	cow, how, brow, crow
21.[p]	paper, people, pimple, pear
22.[b]	bother, brother, bad, bee
23.[t]	ten, two, toilet, tears
24.[d]	bed, bad, dead, dad
25.[k]	kite, speak, kill, cool
26.[g]	glare, glass, good, goose
27.[s]	slow, son, sister
28.[z]	zoo, zebra, zoom, zeal
29.[f]	fish, fly, flee, fight
30.[v]	very, five, vivid, survive
31.[θ]	think, thanks, thick, thoughts
32.[ð]	this, the, those, these
33.[ʃ]	fish, share, shy, shame
34.[ʒ]	pleasure, garage
35.[tʃ]	chair, church, children, chicken
36.[dʒ]	bridge, fridge, judge, juice
37.[tr]	tree, try, tremble, trace
38.[dr]	dream, drain, dragon
39.[ts]	students, nuts, cuts
40.[dz]	beds, aids, woods
41.[l]	like, light, girl, apple
42.[m]	make, room, name, mad
43.[n]	name, know, nose, notice
44.[ŋ]	sing, song, sink
45.[r]	red, right, read, room
46.[h]	how, here, house, home
47.[w]	when, where, we, why
48.[j]	yes, yellow, university

读准了音标和单词之后，就需要练习读词组和句子。因为，在词组和句子中，并不是将音标逐一读出来。和汉语一样，英语也有声调，读起来也有起伏，也有情感，这些都要依赖语音语调，比如单词间的连读、弱读、失去爆破、同化等。很多考生在听雅思听力的时候经常发现自己听到了两个单词，可是翻开原稿一看，竟然有三个单词。那么这种情况是怎么出现的呢？这是因为英语本族语使用者在朗读的时候，有非常自然的连读、弱读、失去爆破等现象，让本来三个单词的短语听起来就像两个一样。为了避免听漏掉音素，有必要了解最基本的发音规则。

连读规则

1. “辅音+元音”型连读

在同一个意群里，如果相邻两词中的前一个词是以辅音结尾，后一个词是以元音开头，这就要将辅音与元音进行连读。比如：

I'm~an~Amercian student.
It~is~an~interesting book.
Have~a look~at~it please.
I called~you half~an~hour~ago.
Not~at~all.

2. “r/re+元音”型连读

如果前一个词是以-r或者-re结尾，后一个词是以元音开头，这时的r或re不但要发/r/，而且还要与后面的元音拼起来连读。

I paid for~it.
There~is a dog under~it.
Here~is a gift for you.
Where~is my seat?
I will love you for ever

3. “辅音+半元音”型连读

英语语音中的/j/和/w/是半元音，如果前一个词是以辅音结尾，后一个词是以半元音，特别是/j/开头，此时也要连读。

Thank~you.
Nice to meet~you.
Did~you pay for it?
Would~you like~a cup~of coffee?
Could~you help me, please?

4. “元音+元音”型连读

如果前一个词以元音结尾，后一个词以元音开头，这两个音往往也要自然而不间断地连读到一起。

I~am a student.
He~is very handsome.
We have to study~English.
How~and why?
It is too~easy.

失去爆破

失去爆破，又叫不完全爆破，即对6个爆破音/p/，/b/，/t/，/d/，/k/，/g/的不完全爆破。就是在某些情况下，对爆破音只需做出发音的口型或留下该音所占的位置，不用将其发出来，稍稍停顿后就发后面的音。

1. “爆破音+爆破音”型

6个爆破音中的任意2个相临时，前一个爆破音会失去爆破，即由相关的发音器官做好这个发音的姿势，稍做停顿后即发后面的爆破音。

re(d) coat
bla(ck) bike
Wha(t) time is it?
an ol(d) pi(c)ture
nex(t) Tuesday
bla(ck) coffee

2. “爆破音+摩擦音”型

如果前面是爆破音，其后紧跟着某些摩擦音（如/f/，/s/，/w/，/t/等），那么前面那个爆破音仅有十分轻微的爆破。

Goo(d) morning.
I wen(t) there.
las(t) night
I don’(t) know.
Le(t) me see.

弱读

弱读是相对于强读或重读而言的。也就是在句子中发音的时候没有被强调或重读的单词或音标。

1. 单词中音的省略

单词内部或词与词之间一个音或几个音的省略。

（1）非重读元音 / e / 和 / i / 的省音较普遍。

如：

secretary / sekrətəri / → / sekrətri /

family / fæmili / → / fæmli /

（2）辅音的省略

在说话语速较快时，可能有几个辅音被省略掉的现象。特别常见的是在两个辅音之间的 / t / 和 / d / 的省略。

如： I used to / aiju:sttu / → / aiju:stu /

2. 句子中词的弱读

通常情况下，冠词、介词、助词、连词等虚词在句子中要弱读。

如： It's made of cheese and eggs.

而一些单词强读的发音和弱读的发音不一样，这也就加大了听力理解的难度。如上例中“will”，“a”，“at”，“is”，“of”和“and”的强读形式分别为/wil/，/ei/，/æt/，/iz/，/əv/和/ænd/。要提高听力理解水平，在平日朗读和说话过程中就必须养成使用弱读的习惯。虽然英语单词强弱读形式不一并且常用词往往有不止一个弱读形式，但只要掌握其构成特点，很容易记住弱读形式的发音。一般语速快时，连读的音连接较紧，语速慢时，连读的音连接较松。

星期三

练习听数字

基数词、序数词、分数、百分数、小数
(cardinal numbers, ordinal numbers, fractions, percentages, decimals)

(一) 基础知识储备

1. 基数词

0	nought/zero/O	20	twenty
1	one	21	twenty-one
2	two	23	twenty-three
3	three	30	thirty
4	four	32	thirty-two
5	five	40	forty
6	six	50	fifty
7	seven	60	sixty
8	eight	70	seventy
9	nine	80	eighty
10	ten	90	ninety
11	eleven	100	one hundred
12	twelve	101	one hundred and one
13	thirteen	156	one hundred and fifty-six
14	fourteen	192	one hundred and ninety-two
15	fifteen	200	two hundred
16	sixteen	700	seven hundred
17	seventeen	900	nine hundred
18	eighteen	1,000	one thousand
19	nineteen	1,000,000	one million
1,001	one thousand and one	3,123,400	three million, one hundred and twenty-three thousand four hundred
1,300	thirteen hundred/one thousand three hundred	8,000,000	eight million
2,000	two thousand	47,000,000	forty-seven million
2,034	two thousand and thirty-four	900,000,000	nine hundred million
6,502	six thousand five hundred and two	1,000,000,000	one billion
38,000	thirty-eight thousand	1,050,000,000	one billion fifty million
45,672	forty-five thousand six hundred and seventy-two	10,000,000,000	ten billion
500,000	five hundred thousand	200,000,000,000	two hundred billion

2. 序数词

first 第一	twelfth 第十二	twenty-third 第二十三
second 第二	thirteenth 第十三	thirtieth 第三十
third 第三	fourteenth 第十四	thirty-first 第三十一
fourth 第四	fifteenth 第十五	fortieth 第四十
fifth 第五	sixteenth 第十六	fiftieth 第五十
sixth 第六	seventeenth 第十七	sixtieth 第六十
seventh 第七	eighteenth 第十八	seventieth 第七十
eighth 第八	nineteenth 第十九	eightieth 第八十
ninth 第九	twentieth 第二十	ninetieth 第九十
tenth 第十	twenty-first 第二十一	(one)hundredth 第一百
eleventh 第十一	twenty-second 第二十二	(one)hundred and first 第一百零一

3. 分数

1/2	one-half/a half
1/3	one-third
3/4	three-fourths
1/5	one-fifth
2/5	two-fifths
7/8	seven-eighths
1/10	one-tenth; a tenth
1/100	one-hundredth; one per cent
1/1000	one-thousandth
1/10000	one ten-thousandth
$2\frac{1}{2}$	two and one half; two and a half
$4\frac{2}{3}$	four and two-thirds

4. 百分数

100%	one hundred per cent
0.5%	point five per cent
0.46%	point four six per cent

5. 小数

2.05	two point nought five; two point O five
6.003	six point nought nought three; six point O O three
78.12	seventy-eight point one two

（二）基础练习

练习1. **Listen to some numbers and write them down in the table.**

1.		2.		3.		4.	
5.		6.		7.		8.	
9.		10.		11.		12.	
13.		14.		15.		16.	
17.		18.		19.		20.	
21.		22.		23.		24.	
25.		26.		27.		28.	
29.		30.		31.		32.	
33.		34.		35.		36.	
37.		38.		39.		40.	
41.		42.		43.		44.	
45.		46.		47.		48.	
49.		50.		51.		52.	
53.		54.		55.		56.	
57.		58.		59.		60.	
61.		62.		63.		64.	
65.		66.		67.		68.	
69.		70.		71.		72.	

英语数字是雅思考试每次必考的考点，理论上讲是送分的题，然而很多考生不能拿到这个部分的分数。其主要原因还是疏于练习。当然，首先还是要掌握英语数字的特点。英语数字和汉语的有本质区别，英语是三位为一个单位，而汉语是四位，所以在英汉转换的时候耗费了时间，也就耽误了听力的速度。因此，在听数字的过程中，一定不能做翻译，或者“心译”。必须用英语思维，否则，听数字将是一个很难的过程。

其实，仔细分析，英语数字是很容易的一部分。基本上只要熟练掌握三位数字的表达，能毫不费力地听出三位数字，那么数字多长都没有关系了。

如：1,234,567,890

要想顺利读出或者听出这个数字，只要会三位数的数字就可以了。这个数字应该读作：

one billion

two hundred and thirty four million

five hundred and sixty seven thousand

eight hundred and ninety

其实，这个数字不管有多少位，都只是 X 百 X 十 X，再加一个单位（billion, million, thousand）就可以了。

在听力过程中，为了回避做翻译，需要做笔记，而且要学会用简写的方式做笔记。比如这个数字的笔记应该是 1b234m567t890。也就是说分别用 billion, million 和 thousand 的首字母来代替这个单位，其他的都是百十个的数字，直接写阿拉伯数字就可以了。甚至还可以给 1～9 每个数字一个速记代码：

1	2	3	4	5	6	7	8	9	0
1	T	TH	FR	FV	SX	SV	E	N	0

这样，就可以完全听到哪个数字写哪个数字，等听力放完之后，再回头来看究竟是多少。接着做下面的练习试一试：

练习 2. Listen and identify the number you hear.

1	A. 15	B. 50	C. 5th
2	A. 180	B. 119	C. 118
3	A. 380	B. 318	C. 319
4	A. 4,560	B. 4,516	C. 4,566
5	A. 17, 890	B. 70,890	C. 17,819
6	A. 730,556	B. 713,566	C. 730,565
7	A. 7,344,600	B. 7,433,600	C. 7,434,600
8	A. 14,500,670	B. 40,500,617	C. 14,500,617
9	A. 590,590,950	B. 519,590,950	C. 519,590,950
10	A. 9,333,450,600	B. 9,333,415,600	C. 9,333,440,600

练习 3. Listen to the dialogue and fill the blanks with a number.

1. His age is ________________.
2. The number of people the auditorium can hold is________________.
3. He has to pay ________________dollars every year.
4. The population of the city is ________________.
5. The number of books in the room is ________________.

电话号码

练习 4. Listen and write down the telephone numbers you hear.

1.		2.	
3.		4.	
5.		6.	
7.		8.	
9.		10.	

11.		12.	
13.		14.	
15.		16.	
17.		18.	
19.		20.	

练习 5. **Listen to the dialogue and fill the blanks with a telephone number.**

1.	
2.	
3.	
4.	
5.	

邮编与产品编码

英语的邮政编码和产品号一般都是数字加字母组成，而中国的邮编只有数字，产品编码也差别甚大，因此，在听到邮编的时候，经常有考生出错。其实，只要稍加练习，就非常容易了。

练习 6. **Listen and write down the postcode you hear.**（下面的邮政编码和产品号都选自雅思听力机经）

1.		2.		3.	
4.		5.		6.	
7.		8.		9.	
10.		11.		12.	
13.		14.		15.	
16.		17.		18.	
19.		20.		21.	
22.		23.		24.	
25.		26.		27.	
28.		29.		30.	

练习 7. **Listen to the dialogue and write down the number you hear.**

1.	
2.	
3.	
4.	
5.	

时 间

时间表达方法：

4:00	four o'clock
04:00	four in the morning/4 a.m
16:00	four in the afternoon/4 p.m
12:00	twelve o'clock/twelve
12:00	twelve in the morning/12 a.m
00:00	twelve at night/12 p.m/midnight
12:15	a quarter past twelve/quarter past twelve/twelve fifteen
02:25	twenty-five past two/ twenty-five minutes past two/ two twenty-five
11:30	half past eleven/ eleven-thirty
12:45	a quarter to one/ quarter to one/ twelve forty-five
Just after five.	刚过 5 点。
It's quarter past.	一刻了。
It is nearly one o'clock.	快一点了。
At a quarter past three in the afternoon.	下午 3 点 15 分。
The time is six forty-five.	现在是 6 点 45 分。
My watch says six thirty.	我的表是 6 点 30 分。
It's five to eight and breakfast's at eight o'clock.	现在差 5 分 8 点整，早餐 8 点钟开始。
The time was 10:35 hours Greenwich Mean Time.	现在是格林威治标准时间 10 点 35 分。
I'll be back at quarter past one.	我 1 点 15 分回来。
By eleven o'clock George was back in his office.	乔治 11 点回到了办公室。

练习 8. Listen and write down the time you hear.

1.		2.	
3.		4.	
5.		6.	
7.		8.	
9.		10.	
11.		12.	
13.		14.	
15.		16.	
17.		18.	
19.		20.	

练习 9. Listen to the dialogue and write down the time you hear.

1	
2	
3	
4	
5	

年月日、星期

月份及简写

一月	January — Jan.	七月	July — Jul.
二月	February — Feb.	八月	August — Aug.
三月	March — Mar.	九月	September — Sep.
四月	April — Apr.	十月	October — Oct.
五月	May — May	十一月	November — Nov.
六月	June — Jun.	十二月	December — Dec.

年份的表达

年份一般用基数词表示，写时可以用阿拉伯数字。读时一般先读前两位，再读后两位；整百的年份一般以 hundred 为单位。

1840 年读为 eighteen forty，而 1900 年则可直接以 hundred 为单位；2000 年可以以 hundred 为单位，也可以以 thousand 为单位。

例如：

1840 年　eighteen forty
1900 年　nineteen hundred
1992 年　nineteen ninety-two
2000 年　twenty hundred/ two thousand
2003 年　twenty zero three

年代表示方法

1980's，指的是 20 世纪 80 年代（1980—1989 年），读作 nineteen eighties.
另外还有 early eighties、mid eighties 和 late eighties 的说法。

日期的表达

5 月 14 日可以读作：May the 14th，也可以读作：the fourteenth of May. 写作 May 14th。但要特别注意的是：在英式英语中，日期在前，月份在后，即顺序为“日月年”；但在美式英语中，则月份在前，日期在后，即顺序为“月日年”。

例如：08-04-96 在英式英语中是表示 April eighth, 1996，而在美式英语中，则表示 August 4th, 1996。

星期及简写

星期一	Monday — Mon.
星期二	Tuesday — Tue.
星期三	Wednesday — Wed.
星期四	Thursday — Thu.
星期五	Friday — Fri.
星期六	Saturday — Sat.
星期日	Sunday — Sun.

练习 10. Listen to the following expressions and write them down.

1.		2.	
3.		4.	
5.		6.	
7.		8.	
9.		10.	
11.		12.	
13.		14.	
15.		16.	
17.		18.	
19.		20.	

练习 11. Listen to the dialogue and fill the blanks.

1. Today is ________________.
2. I would leave Australia on________________.
3. Today is Tuesday, ________________.
4. The deadline of our thesis is ________________.
5. My brother is going back to China on________________.

钱 币

美国货币	英国货币
美国货币由美元 dollar 和美分 cent 组成，one dollar=100 cents 其纸币（bill）有 1；2；5；10；20；50；100 美元等面值 硬币（coin）有一美分（或 a penny）、五美分（或 a nickel）、十美分（或 a dime）和二十五美分（或 a quarter）等 在数字前加$表示美元，如：$700 表示七百美元；在数字后加 C 表示美分，如：80C 表示 80 美分；表示由美元和美分组成的钱数时，常用$表示，如：$6.50	英国货币由英镑（pound）和便士（pence）组成，100 pence=1 pound 纸币 notes 有 5；10；20；50 镑等面值 硬币，有一便士、二便士、五便士、十便士、二十便士、五十便士和一镑等 在数字前加￡表示英镑，如：￡600 为 600 英镑；在数字后加 P 表示便士，如：5P 表示五便士；表示由英镑和便士组成的钱数时通常不说出 pence，如 6 镑 50 便士可说成￡6.50 或 six pounds and fifty

"钱"在英语中的10种表达法

1	rent	土地、房屋、机器等的租费
2	tuition	学费
3	tip	小费
4	postage	邮费
5	freight	运费，指海运、空运、陆运的费用
6	fee	医生、律师及其他职业的佣金、会费、手续费、停车费等
7	fare	搭乘公共汽车、出租车火车等交通工具开销的费用
8	charge	要价，常用复数形式。主要指用于一次性劳务收取的费用
9	admission	入场费
10	expenses	花费，开支

钱数的读法

$6	six dollars
$0.5	half a dollar/ point five dollar/ 50 cents
$2.50	two point five dollars
£8	eight pounds
£0.5	fifty pence/ half a pound
£3.50	three pounds fifty

练习 12. Listen and write down what you hear.

1.		2.	
3.		4.	
5.		6.	
7.		8.	
9.		10.	

练习 13. Listen to the dialogue and finish the tasks.

1. How much is the rent every month? ________________
2. How much should he pay?________________
3. How much is the tip?________________
4. How much is the postage?________________
5. How much is the subway fare in London?________________
6. How much was he charged?________________
7. How much is the admission for the circus?________________
8. How much is the expense of studying in UK every year?________________
9. How much is the rent to rent a car for a week?________________
10. How much is the fee?________________

星期四 单词拼写

今天的学习任务是练习听地名、人名及字母拼写。

地　名

（一）基础知识储备

地名是雅思听力必考的考点。而且，考核的范围非常广，从国家、国籍、城市名到街道、门牌号。

世界重要国家、国籍和首都，以及重要城市都是非常常见的考点。但考试的时候不只是考一个地名的拼写。比如听力原稿中一个人说他出生在新德里，但题目却是要求填国籍（印度），很多考试虽然能听懂新德里，但却不能填出准确的答案，非常遗憾。但这个问题就不是听力的问题，而是知识面的问题，所以为了应对这样的考题，需要对全世界主要国家、国籍、首都和重要城市有一个全面的了解。

首先考生要记住下面这个表格——世界重要国家、国籍和首都，然后在世界地图上找到它们，做到"心中有图"，听的时候也就胸有成竹了。

国　家	国　籍	首　都
China	Chinese	Beijing
Japan	Japanese	Tokyo
South Korea	South Korean	Seoul
Thailand	Thai	Bangkok
Vietnam	Vietnamese	Hanoi
Malaysia	Malaysian	Kuala Lumpur
Indonesia	Indonesian	Jakarta
Pakistan	Pakistani	Islamabad
Philippines	Philippine	Manila
India	Indian	New Delhi
The USA	American	Washington
Canada	Canadian	Ottawa
Mexico	Mexican	Mexico City
Brazil	Brazilian	Brasilia
Argentina	Argentine	Buenos Aires

（续）

国　家	国　籍	首　都
Italy	Italian	Rome
Sweden	Swedish	Stockholm
Switzerland	Swiss	Bern
Norway	Norwegian	Oslo
Finland	Finnish	Helsinki
Denmark	Danish	Copenhagen
Germany	German	Berlin
France	French	Paris
Britain	British	London
Spain	Spanish	Madrid
Russia	Russian	Moscow
Austria	Austrian	Vienna
Greece	Greek	Athens
Poland	Polish	Warsaw
Australia	Australian	Canberra
New Zealand	New Zealander	Wellington

U. K.	Liverpool 利物浦 Manchester 曼彻斯特 Sheffield 谢菲尔德 Birmingham 伯明翰 Coventry 考文垂 Leeds 利兹 Scotland 苏格兰	Glasgow 格拉斯哥 Edinburgh 爱丁堡 Wales 威尔士 Cardiff 加的夫 North Ireland 北爱尔兰 Belfast 贝尔法斯特
Australia	Canberra 堪培拉 Queensland 昆士兰州 Brisbane 布里斯班 New South Wales 新南威尔士州 Sydney 悉尼	Adelaide 阿德莱德 Victoria 维多利亚州 Melbourne 墨尔本 Perth 珀斯 Great Barrier Reef 大堡礁
USA	Washington 华盛顿 New York 纽约 Atlanta 亚特兰大	Seattle 西雅图 Los Angeles/L.A. 洛杉矶 Chicago 芝加哥
Canada	Ottawa 渥太华 Victoria 维多利亚 Vancouver 温哥华	Ontario 安大略省 Toronto 多伦多 Quebec 魁北克省 Montreal 蒙特利尔

（二）基础练习

练习 1. Listen and write down the addresses.

1.		2.		3.	
4.		5.		6.	
6.		8.		9.	
10.		11.		12.	
13.		14.		15.	
16.		17.		18.	
19.		20.		21.	
22.		23.		24.	
25.		26.		27.	
28.		29.		30.	

练习 2. Listen to the dialogue and fill the blanks.

1. My address is ____________________.
2. I live on ____________________.
3. The ticket should be sent to ____________________.
4. He is at ____________________.
5. The apartment is on ____________________.

人　名

（一）基础知识储备

雅思听力中人名是必考的考点，一般情况下，如果碰到的人名比较生僻就一定会有拼写，但是如果是常用人名，就不会按字母拼写出来，因此，要掌握最常用人名的拼写。

常用人名

Abraham	亚伯拉罕	Jim	吉姆
Adam	亚当	Joe	乔
Alex	亚历克斯	John	约翰
Alexander	亚历山大	Johnny	约翰尼
Alan	艾伦	Kenny	肯尼
Andrew	安德鲁	Kevin	凯文
Andy	安迪	Lawrence	劳伦斯
Arthur	亚瑟	Lee	李
Ben	本	Leo	雷欧
Bill	比尔	Mark	马克
Bob	鲍伯	Mars	马尔斯

Brian	布莱恩	Michael	迈克尔
Bruce	布鲁斯	Mike	麦克
Carl	卡尔	Neil	尼尔
Charles	查尔斯	Oliver	奥利弗
Chris	克里斯	Oscar	奥斯卡
Christian	克里斯蒂安	Paul	保罗
Daniel	丹尼尔	Peter	彼得
Dennis	丹尼斯	Richard	理查德
Douglas	道格拉斯	Robert	罗伯特
David	大卫	Robinson	罗宾逊
Edward	爱德华	Roger	罗杰
Eric	埃里克	Roy	罗伊
Frank	弗兰克	Sam	萨姆
Franklin	富兰克林	Scott	斯考特
Fred	弗瑞德	Sean	肖恩
George	乔治	Simon	西蒙
Howard	霍华德	Steven	史蒂文
Henry	亨利	Stuart	斯图亚特
Jack	杰克	Terry	特里
Jackson	杰克逊	Tom	汤姆
Jacob	雅各布	Thomas	托马斯
James	詹姆士	Tony	托尼
Jason	詹森	Tyler	泰勒
Jeffery	杰弗瑞	William	威廉
Jerry	杰瑞		

（二）基础练习

练习 3．Listen and write down the names your hear.

1.		2.		3.	
4.		5.		6.	
7.		8.		9.	
10.		11.		12.	
13.		14.		15.	

练习 4．Listen to the dialogue and fill the blanks.

1．His name is ____________________.
2．The applicant's name is ____________________.
3．The applicant's name is ____________________.
4．The name of the caller is ____________________.
5．The applicant's name is ____________________.

星期五

听写

听写是听力基本功训练非常有用的一种方法。通过听写能迅速提高考生听力的辨音能力，训练考生获取细节信息的能力；做笔记的能力；培养考生集中注意力的能力等。总之，听写练习能在短期内让考生的听力基本功上一个很大的台阶。因此，我们特别安排一天的时间来学习听写的方法，我们从单词、词组、句子、段落多个层面进行听写练习，以期为考生听后面的雅思听力题目做一个很好的铺垫。

单词听写

练习 1. **Listen and write down the words you hear.**

单词		听写关注	单词		听写关注
1.		单词内部连读	16.		单词重音
2.		不发音的字母	17.		拼写准确
3.		不发音的字母	18.		单词重音
4.		不发音的字母	19.		单词重音
5.		单词重音	20.		双写
6.		音准	21.		清辅音浊化
7.		单词重音	22.		单词重音
8.		清辅音浊化	23.		单词重音
9.		末尾清辅音	24.		同音词
10.		不发音的字母	25.		单词重音
11.		外来词发音	26.		双写
12.		单词内部弱读	27.		双写
13.		单词内部弱读	28.		双写
14.		英美拼写区别	29.		清辅音浊化
15.		单词重音	30.		单词内部失去爆破

词组听写

练习 2. Listen and write down the expressions you hear.

Expressions		听写关注
1.		失去爆破；缩写
2.		否定；失去爆破；缩写
3.		缩写
4.		失去爆破
5.		连读
6.		失去爆破
7.		连读
8.		失去爆破
9.		缩写；连读
10.		连读

句子听写

练习 3. Listen and write down the sentences you hear. You will listen to the sentences twice.

1.	
2.	
3.	
4.	
5.	
6.	
7.	
8.	
9.	
10.	

段落听写

（一）整段听写

练习 4. Listen to a short passage introducing the city of Oxford, write down every word you hear. You can listen to the recording for three times.

听前提示：

听力录音将会播放三遍。第一遍考生应该仔细倾听，尽可能抓住文章大意。第二遍听的时候，考生应该记下尽可能多的信息，要灵活使用速记技巧。第三遍就是检查并补全信息。

Oxford is

（二）听段落、补全空格

练习 5. Listen to the recording and fill in the blanks according to what you hear.

INFORMATION FOR REFEREES

References should be supplied in ❶____________________. Referees should comment on the ❷____________________ and general ❸____________________ for the proposed programme of study.

Referees should also supply any other information they consider to ❹____________________ the candidate's application and where they have knowledge of ❺____________________. It would be helpful if they could indicate❻____________________ achieved.

All references must be received by the relevant ❼____________________.

The reference supplied will be treated as ❽____________________, subject to the provisions of the UK ❾____________________ of 1998. If the candidate requests to see the reference, we may need to provide a ⑩ ____________.

（三）听段落，补全大意

练习 6. Listen to the recording and complete the summary of the article you hear.

Bodleian Libraries	is the integrated library service of the University of Oxford. It comprises nearly ❶ ____________ libraries. There are major research libraries and libraries attached to ❷ ____________ , ❸ ____________and other ❹ ____________ of the University.
The Bodleian Library	is the ❺ ____________ largest in the UK after the British Library. It has ❻ _______ miles of occupied shelving, 29 reading rooms and ❼ ____________ places for readers.
College Libraries	Every College has its own library, often consisting of a modern, working library and ❽ ____________ collections.
Search Oxford Libraries Online	offers a ❾ ____________ and delivery solution for quickly accessing Oxford's main library information resources regardless of ❿ ____________ .
Oxford Libraries Information System	All Oxford libraries participate in the ⓫ ____________ .
E-resources	University libraries share an extensive range of e-resources across all ⓬ ____________ .
Oxford Digital Library	Oxford is actively involved in developing electronic information, including ⓭ _______ and ⓮ ____________ .
Oxford University Libraries A-Z	The University also houses many ⓯ ____________ libraries.

星期六

听对话

今天的任务很简单，是 20 组对话练习。

练习：Listen to the dialogue and finish the tasks.

Dialogue ❶

What's Watalabe's problem?

A. He has a stiff neck.

B. He has too much work to do.

C. He doesn't like coffee break.

Dialogue ❷

What does Fiona suggest in the end?

A. She suggests having some discussion.

B. She advises calling it a good day.

C. She thinks they should stop working that day.

Dialogue ❸

Today, Truman is not going to

A. meet a friend at the airport.

B. have lunch with his friend.

C. talk to his professor.

Dialogue ❹

Why didn't Brain show up today?

A. Because he was sick.

B. Because his parents died.

C. Because of his sister.

How is brain's sister now?

A. She is fine now.

B. She is still out of conscious.

C. She is not badly hurt.

Dialogue ❺

What is Roger doing?

A. He is shopping.

B. He is playing computer games.

C. He is tied to something.

Why did Jill let Roger go on what he is doing?

A. Because she is very nice to Roger.

B. Because she is happy about the gift.

C. Because she feels sorry for bother Roger.

Dialogue ❻

What are they going to do tonight?

A. They are going home.

B. They are going to eat at school.

C. They are going to have group study.

Dialogue ❼

What happened between Bush and Mark?

A. Bush turned Mark's nose up.

B. Mark refused to help Bush.

C. They were not in talking mood.

What will Bush do?

A. He will forget Mark.

B. He will forget Mark's name.

C. He will let it go.

Dialogue ❽

What was wrong with his face?

A. He hurt himself when get shaved.

B. He got cut by a knife.

C. He has long beard.

What shouldn't he do next time?

A. Shave in a shower.

B. Press hard.

C. Use some cream before shaving.

Dialogue ❾

The man cannot get a raise because his company ________________

Dialogue ⑩

What can't the man take a vocation?

A. Because he had a two-day holiday recently.

B. Because he will be fired.

C. Because the company gives him too much work to do.

What will the man do soon?

A. He will talk to the manager.

B. He will have a meeting with the manager.

C. He will talk about his problem in the meeting the next day.

Dialogue ⑪

According to the man, how should the woman behave in the interview?

A. She should be confident.

B. She should tell them her experiences.

C. She should make the interviewer know that she is cooperative.

Dialogue ⑫

What are they talking about?

A. They are talking about the thermometer.

B. They are talking about the terribly hot weather.

C. They are talking about what to do after dark.

Dialogue ⑬

Where are the two speakers?

A. They are in a shopping mall.

B. They are in the man's house.

C. They are in the woman's house.

Dialogue ⑭

What will the male speaker do on the fifteenth?

A. He will be in a meeting.

B. He will attend a lecture.

C. He will have lunch with the woman.

Dialogue ⑮

The man will go to the following places except

A. shops.

B. supermarket.

C. library.

What will the man buy?

A. vegetables

B. bacon

C. beer

D. cake

E. books

Dialogue ⑯

What will the man do in the coming two weeks?

A. Go to Japan.

B. Have a new project.

C. Meet the woman.

Dialogue ⑰

What's wrong with the man?

A. He had a car accident.

B. He was overcharged.

C. the Consumer Protection Agency didn't help.

Dialogue ⑱

What are the woman's chances of getting the job?

A. Very possible.

B. There is no hope.

C. Do not know.

Dialogue ⑲

What is Douglas's new home number?

A. 6735667

B. 7645984

C. 3984059

Dialogue ⑳

They seat: 1 ____________

The woman's order: Food: 2 ____________

Drink:3 ____________

The man's order: Food: 4 ____________

Drink:5 ____________

星期日

听新闻

今天我们为您准备了 10 组新闻练习。

练习 1

1. Which of the following is the best title for the news story ?

A. Northerners and southerners are going to vote for unity in Sudan.

B. South Sudanese Want Independence from North.

C. Southerners have suffered too much as a unified country.

D. There will be a war between the south and the north.

2. Which of the following is NOT TRUE according to the news story ?

A. Many citizens in South Sudan don't care about the coming divorce.

B. Most southerners feel discriminated against and marginalized by their Muslim-Arab Compatriots.

C. According to southerners, if there is a war, it will be initiated from the northerners.

D. Southerners believe that development and prosperity will come to their region if they are on their own.

练习 2

1. What does the dance of Gurrir Gurrir people describe?

A. The dance describes Australia's most important festivals of indigenous art.

B. The dance describes the Aboriginees' ancient spirits.

C. The dance describes events related with a devastating tropical cyclone in 1974.

D. The dance describes the diversity of indigenous culture and the Warmun artistic tradition.

2. Where does the exhibition take place?

A. In Sydney.
B. In South Wales.
C. In Darwin.
D. In Warrmarn-Kija.

练习 3

1. Why did workers in London walk out ?

A. Because there was a strike in London.

B. Because the major transport routes had been closed down and transport links had been turned into chaos.

C. Because they were not prepared to be pushed around.

D. Because they believed proposed job cuts would hurt the service and create safety risks.

2. Who is Crow?

A. a worker　　**B.** a tube driver

C. British Union leader　　**D.** a Londoner

练习 4

1. Which of the following cause greater demands on the planet's water resources?

A. A soaring world population and climate change.

B. Climate change and greater demands for food.

C. A soaring world population.

D. Both B and C.

2. Who is the World Bank Water Sector Manager?

A. Andersen　　**B.** Julia Bucknall

C. Inger Andersen　　**D.** Julian Bucknall

3. Which of the following is the percentage of hydropower potential located in developing countries?

A. only 23%　　**B.** at least 23%　　**C.** about 43%　　**D.** more than 3%

练习 5

1. When did the Deepwater Horizon drill rig explode?

A. In April.　　**B.** In mid-August.

C. In mid-July.　　**D.** In late April.

2. How many barrels of oil did the U.S. scientists estimate leaked from the damaged well?

A. 1 billion　　**B.** nearly 5 million

C. more than 1 million　　**D.** at least 5 million

练习 6

1. Britain's new coalition government has passed an _________ after warning the state of the country's finances is much worse than expected .

2. The apartments are dark and damp and the estate suffers from high levels of _________, _________ and _________ .

3. The apartment blocks were due to be _________ and _________, but the money has run out.

练习 7

1. The killing of the British personnel has raised more questions in Britain about the _________.

2. The death of five brave soldiers in a single incident is a terrible and tragic loss and I want to _________ to their professionalism and to their courage and service.

3. Britain is the second highest _________ to the NATO force in Afghanistan.

练习 8

1. Britain's Queen Elizabeth II has formally opened _________ in a traditional ceremony full of pomp and circumstance.

2. Britain is estimated to be facing more than _________ in debt.

3. On the new Conservative-Liberal Democrat legislative agenda was the topic of _________.

练习 9

1. The plan was to develop a _________ dollar iron ore facility inside the Woomera Prohibited Area, a military testing base in South Australia.

2. This latest decision could _________ relations between Canberra and Beijing.

练习 10

1. Nearly 100 world leaders met at a _________ at the United Nations Tuesday to put their political weight behind achieving a global climate treaty later this year.

2. Mr. Ban said a successful deal would be one that includes _________ and _________ support for emerging countries.

3. China's President Hu Jintao announced plans to cut emissions significantly by 2020, and to vigorously develop _________ and _________ energy.

4周攻克

雅思听力周计划

第二周　题型渗透听力策略

本周的学习任务是针对雅思听力考试的各类题型的渗透策略。

第一周	每日学习内容
星期一	填表题（Forms/Notes/Tables Completion）
星期二	多选题（Multiple Choice）
星期三	填图题（Labeling）
星期四	完成句子（Sentence Completion）
星期五	补全题（Summary Completion）
星期六	配对题（Matching）
星期日	简答题（Short Answer Questions）

星期一
填表题（Forms/Notes/Tables Completion）

一、题型介绍

In this task type, candidates are required to fill in gaps in an outline of part or of all of the listening text. The outline will focus on the main ideas/facts in the text. In all cases, note form can be used when completing the gaps. This means that articles, auxiliary verbs etc. may be omitted when they are not necessary for the meaning. The summary is written in connected sentences and so it must be grammatically correct.

The outline may be

1. a form: often used to record factual details such as names.

2. a set of notes: used to summarise any type of information using the layout to show how different items relate to one another.

3. a table: used as a way of summarising information which relates to clear categories – e.g. place/time/price.

In this case, they should keep to the word limit stated in the instructions. Candidates do not have to change the words from the recording in any way. Candidates should read the instructions very carefully as the number of words or numbers they should use to fill the gaps will vary. A word limit is given, for example, "NO MORE THAN THREE WORDS AND/OR A NUMBER". Candidates are penalised for writing more than the stated number of words, and candidates should check this word limit carefully for each task. Contracted words will not be tested. Hyphenated words count as single words.

This task type focuses on the main points which a listener would naturally record in this type of situation.

填表题是要求考生根据所听内容完成一个表格、便笺或列表。一般情况下，考生需要填写的答案是地名、人名、数字或其他具体信息。字数要求是 NO MORE THAN THREE WORDS AND/OR A NUMBER。一般不填虚词，而且要求答案从语法上是正确的。考生可以根据听力原文进行填空，也就是不需要变换词形，也不要使用缩写答题。

二、题型练习

Example 1

Questions 1-7

Complete the notes below.

*Write **NO MORE THAN THREE WORDS AND/OR A NUMBER** for each answer.*

MOVIES
Name: 1. ________
Address: 2. ________
Postcode: 3. ________
Nationality: 4. ________
Time period: 5. ________
Types of movies: 6. ________
and 7. ________

Example 2

Questions 1-9

Complete the notes below.

*Write **NO MORE THAN THREE WORDS AND/OR A NUMBER** for each answer.*

BANK LOAN APPLICATION FORM
Name: 1. ________
Address: 2. ________
Office number: 3. ________
Birthday: 4. ________
Occupation 5. ________
Annual salary 6. ________
Marital status 7. ________
Occupation of spouse: 8. ________
Purpose of loan: 9. ________

Example 3

Questions 1-10

Complete the form below.

*Write **NO MORE THAN THREE WORDS AND/OR A NUMBER** for each answer.*

INVESTIGATION INTO A BURGLARY	
Name	1. Anna ________
Date of birth	2. ________
Postcode	3. ________
Nationality	4. ________
stayed in UK for	5. ________
Number of roommate	6. ________
Burglar came from	7. ________
Stuff missing	8. ________
Serial number of computer	9. ________
The color of purse	10. ________

星期二

多选题（Multiple Choice）

一、题型介绍

In this task type, there is a question followed by three possible answers, or the beginning of a sentence followed by three possible sentence endings. Candidates are required to choose the one correct answer A, B or C.

Sometimes candidates are given a longer list of possible answers and told that they have to choose more than one. In this case they should read the question carefully to check how many answers are required.

This task type is used to test a wide range of skills. It may require the candidate to have a detailed understanding of specific points or an overall understanding of the main points of the listening text.

多选题是要求考生根据听力内容从三个选项中选择一个答题。如果选项超过四个，考生要特别注意，可能是该题有两个选项。一般情况下，选择题的答案不会直接给出，也就是说如果某个选项和听力原稿完全相同，这样的选项往往是一个干扰项。大多数答案都是通过同义词替换等方式隐藏在听力原稿中。因此，在练习听力的时候，考生要特别关注同义词表达。

二、题型练习

Example 1

Questions 1-4

*Choose the correct letter, **A**, **B**, **C** or **D**.*

1. The party will be held on
   A. Friday.　　**B.** Saturday.　　**C.** Sunday.
2. George says he will arrive at
   A. 6:30.　　**B.** 6:45.　　**C.** 7:00.
3. What will George bring to the party?
   A. wine　　**B.** beer　　**C.** cookies　　**D.** fruit juice
4. What instrument does Janice suggest George to bring?
   A. piano　　**B.** flute　　**C.** guitar

Example 2

Questions 1-5

*Choose the correct letter, **A, B** or **C**.*

1. What method is Lily going to use to do her research?
   A. class observation
   B. questionnaires
   C. interview
2. How will Lily get teachers' opinion?
   A. Observe their classes.
   B. Use questionnaires.
   C. Interview them.
3. Why does Lily think observing classes is not good?
   A. It is not reliable.
   B. It is a very good method.
   C. The students don't like her sitting in the classroom.
4. Hans, project is
   A. the same as Lily's.
   B. about the same field.
   C. totally different from Lily's.
5. Why does Han think group work is not good?
   A. Students have to work with each other.
   B. It defeats the purpose of it.
   C. It is unnecessary.

Example 3

Questions 1-7

*Choose the correct letter, **A, B** or **C**.*

1. When did May go to the library?
   A. Wednesday
   B. Thursday
   C. Friday
2. May is looking at Chimpanzees because
   A. she is particularly interested in this animal.
   B. she wanted to check what she has seen in a documentary.
   C. she happened to get the resources available.
3. According to May, chimpanzees can
   A. make tools for any purposes.
   B. cooperate with other chimpanzees to hunt.

C. understand all human languages.

4. Chimpanzees dig into termite mounds with sticks, because they
   A. like playing with termites.
   B. think this can help them to get food.
   C. hate termites who often bite them.
5. How do chimpanzees show their spiritual life?
   A. They appreciate beautiful sceneries.
   B. They take turtles as their babies.
   C. They show their happiness by mourning.
6. What can Chimpanzees use to communicate?
   A. sounds
   B. body language
   C. sticks
7. How many signs did Washoe learned eventually?
   A. 51
   B. 151
   C. 800

星期三

填图题（Labeling）

一、题型介绍

In this task type, candidates are required to complete labels on a visual. The answers are usually selected from a list on the question paper. Candidates should transfer the letter of the option they have selected to the answer sheet in the time allowed.

The visual may be a diagram (e.g. a piece of equipment), a set of pictures, a plan (e.g. of a building), a map (e.g. of part of a town).

This task type assesses the ability to understand, for example, a description of a place, and to relate this to a visual representation. This may include being able to follow language expressing spatial relationships and directions (e.g. straight on/through the far door).

填图题是要求考生根据听力内容从一系列选项中选择代号填充一个图表，或一套图片；也可能是一个蓝图或地图。建议考生熟练掌握表示方位和空间关系的英语表达，避免误填。

二、题型练习

Example 1: Label the plan below.

1. ________________
2. ________________
3. ________________
4. ________________
5. ________________

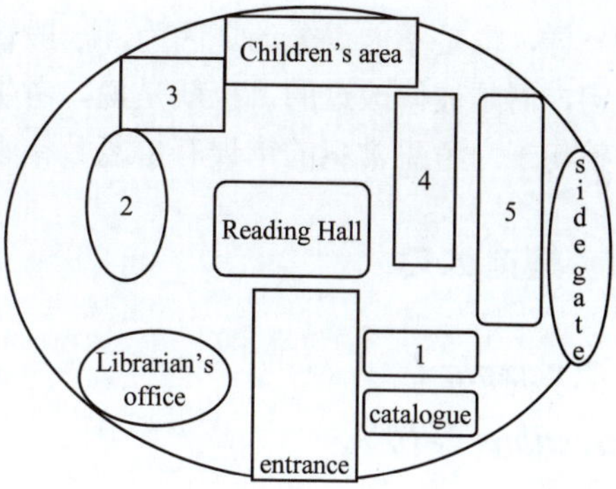

Example 2: Match the numbers and the places.

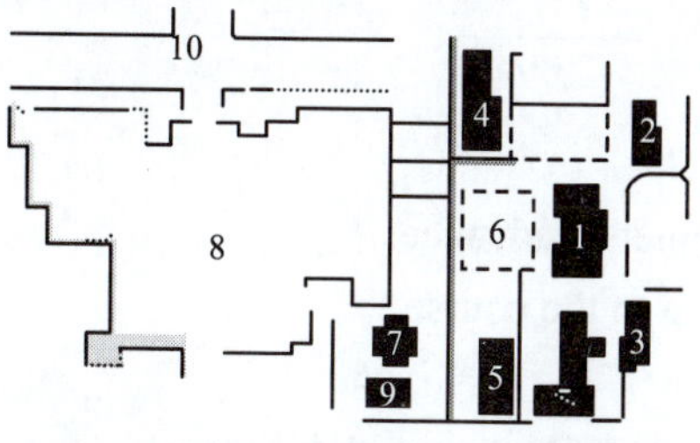

A. Library
B. Conference building
C. Canteen
D. Garden
E. Café
F. Administration building
G. Side gate
H. Playground
I. Dormitory
J. Teaching building

星期四

完成句子（Sentence Completion）

一、题型介绍

In this task type, candidates are required to read a set of sentences summarising key information from all the listening text or from one part of it. They have to complete a gap in each sentence using information from the listening text. They usually have to write no more than three words and/or a number.

完成句子是雅思听力考试必考的题型。考生需要根据自己听到的内容补充完整一个句子。使其语义完整、语法正确，并且符合听力内容。考生需要在空格中填上一个数字或者一个不超过三个单词的答案。在完成这种类型题目的时候，考生要特别留意，所填答案应能让不完整的句子变得完整，即语法必须正确。如果语法不正确，即便是所填答案和听力原稿一模一样，也是不能得分的。因为，一般情况下，考生所看到的不完整的句子不是听力原稿的原句，而是被修改过的，也就是说，考生要根据自己对听力的理解，获取关键信息，并补充完整句子。考生常犯的错误有单复数错误、时态错误、数据混淆等。

二、题型练习

Example 1

Questions 1-10

Complete the sentences below.

Write ***NO MORE THAN THREE WORDS*** *for each answer.*

1. Age of his son: ________.
2. Many parents think their kids need to be with ________.
3. The course is for the kids aging from ________to ________.
4. The course is a ________ course run by parents.
5. Parents who want to attend need to get ________.
6. The teacher suggests the parent ________ the center in advance.
7. The kid needs to be more ________ when they go to the course.
8. The total cost for the kid is: ________.
9. How much does the parent need to pay every month if he goes with his son: ________.
10. The parent needs to take the register in the center from ________ to ________.

Example 2

Questions 1-8

Listen to the following telephone conversation between a hotel receptionist and a person trying to make a booking. The line is bad but the receptionist has the telephone skills to deal with this problem.

Complete the sentences below.

Write ***NO MORE THAN THREE WORDS*** *for each answer.*

1. The name of the customer ________.
2. The customer will check in on ________.
3. The customer reserved ________.
4. The customer needs ________ food.
5. Special food can be provided by ________.
6. The number of guests ________.
7. The date the customer is going to check out ________.
8. The customer reserved an alarm call at ________.

Example 3

SECTION 1 *Questions 1-10*

Questions 1-6

The caller is requesting information about making a group booking. There will be up to __1__ people in the group.

The restaurant caters for groups with a maximum of __2__ people.

The group includes people with different dietary requirements: __3__, meat eaters, gluten-free and __4__ allergies.

There are 4 different menus. The most expensive option is menu __5__ which costs __6__.

Questions 7-10

The menu includes a selection of __7__, a choice from 3 main courses, __8__ of wine per person, dessert and coffee.

BOOKING FORM
NAME: ____9____
E-MAIL: hb0470@freemail.com
TEL NO: ____10____

星期五

补全题（Summary Completion）

一、题型介绍

In this task type, candidates are required to read a set of sentences summarising key information from all the listening text or from one part of it. They have to complete a gap in each sentence using information from the listening text. A word limit is given, for example, "NO MORE THAN THREE WORDS AND/OR A NUMBER". Candidates are penalised for writing more than the stated number of words. (Candidates should check this word limit carefully for each task). Contracted words will not be tested. Hyphenated words count as single words. The words that the candidates use for their answers do not have to be taken directly from the listening text.

This task type focuses on the ability to identify the key information in a listening text. Candidates have to understand functional relationships such as cause and effect.

补全摘要是雅思听力难度最大的听力题型。该题型要求考生在听懂听力内容的前提下，提取关键词，完成对听力原稿的摘要。也就是说考生听到的听力原稿和阅读的摘要不完全一样，需要考生一边听，一边总结听力内容，并提取关键信息，组织语言来作答。

二、题型练习

Example 1

Complete the summary below.

In most Western countries, it is __1__ for children to receive primary education. Primary education generally begins when children are __2__ years old. The division between primary and secondary education generally occurs at about __3__ years of age. Primary education is provided in __4__ , until they complete it and move on to secondary schooling. The major goals of primary education are achieving __5__ and __6__ amongst all their students, as well as establishing foundations in __7__ and other social sciences.

Example 2

Complete the summary below.

When buying a house, consumers have to deal with __1__, solicitors, surveyors, __2__, __3__ and others. When they want to buy a property, they need to approach a __4__ to help with the purchase. Generally over the period of a mortgage the borrower will pay back nearly ___5___ as much as they borrowed! Until recently nearly all home buyers would have used a ___6___ to provide them with a mortgage, and many Societies converting to or being taken over by ___7___. Many banks now offer competitive rates and the market has been joined by other lenders such as ___8___ or ___9___ who can compete by keeping down the ___10___ incurred by having a high street presence.

Example 3

Complete the summary below.

Richard Trevithick was the first man to combine the ___1___ and wagon-ways In 1803, he designed a steam engine that could run on ___2___ . In ___3___, his engine pulled wagons carrying 18 tonnes of iron ore and 70 men for ___4___. Britain's railways were taken into state control during ___5___, and until 1996 they were ___6___ again. Today there are 25 train operators who run the services. Network Rail, an ___7___ company is one of them; there are also a number of ___8___ organizations that are involved in running the railways. So the railway system is very developed, according to statistics, only ___9___ British trains are late, and there is a very good network called the Rail Passenger Council which deals with ___10___ and will also give a lot of advice on problems.

星期六

配对题（Matching）

一、题型介绍

In this task type, candidates are required to match a numbered list of items from the listening text to a set of options on the question paper. The set of options may be criteria of some kind. Many variations of this task type are possible with regards the type of options to be matched.

This task type assesses the skill of listening for detail. It assesses whether a candidate can understand information given in a conversation on an everyday topic such as different types of hotel or guest house accommodation. It also assesses the ability to follow a conversation involving interaction between two people. It may also be used to assess candidates' ability to recognise relationships and connections between facts in the listening text.

配对题是一种选择题，即要求考生从几个选项中分别选择相应答案作答。与多选题的区别是，多选题是三选一或五选二，而配对题是多个选项对多个题目。该题型考核考生筛选类似信息的能力。往往选项都是互相干扰或容易混淆的。因此，考生需要仔细倾听，并且做笔记，反复比对，最终确定答案。

二、题型练习

Example 1

Questions 1-4

Which hotel matches each description?

*Choose your answers from the box and write the correct letter, **A-D**, next to questions 1-4.*

Hotels

A. The Skypass Hotel
B. Hilton House
C. The Emperor's
D. The Big Apple

1. __________ is in a rural area.
2. __________ only opened recently.
3. __________ offers facilities for business functions.
4. __________ has an indoor swimming pool.

Example 2

What does George tell his tutor about each of the following course options?

A. He'll definitely do it. **B.** He may or may not do it. **C.** He won't do it.

*Write the correct letter, **A**, **B** or **C** next to questions 6-10.*

You may choose any letter more than once.

6. Mass Media

7. Children's Studies

8. Western Culture

9. Overseas Students' Identity

10. Introduction to Digitalization

三、配对题常用表达法

Will definitely do it

That would fit in really well.

Put me down for that.

I'll go for that.

I'll sign up for that.

That sounds perfect.

That one's for me.

I'd definitely like to do that.

May or may not do it

I'll think about that one.

I'll consider it.

I don't really know about that.

It depends on the course teacher.

I might wait to decide.

It sounds interesting but I'm.

worried it might be difficult.

I'm not sure – I'll sleep on it.

Won't do it

I'd rather not take that.

That sounds dull.

That's not really relevant for me.

I don't think I like the sound of that.

I've decided I'd rather do

something completely new.

I'll forget about that one then.

I think I'll give that a miss.

星期日

简答题（Short Answer Questions）

一、题型介绍

In this task type, candidates are required to read a question to which they have to write a short answer using information from the listening text. A word limit is given, for example, "NO MORE THAN THREE WORDS AND/OR A NUMBER". Candidates are penalised for writing more than the stated number of words. (Candidates should check this word limit carefully for each task.) Contracted words will not be tested. Hyphenated words count as single words. Sometimes candidates are given a question which asks them to list two or three points.

This task type focuses on the ability to listen for concrete facts—such as places, prices or times—given in the listening text.

简答题要求考生根据听力内容用一个数字或不超过三个单词的简短答案来回答问题。简答题是难度较大的一个题型。考生需要在听懂听力内容的基础上，提取关键词来作答。

二、题型练习

Example 1

Questions 1-7

Answer the following questions.

*Write **NO MORE THAN THREE WORDS** for each answer.*

1. What product did the customer buy? __________
2. What model is it? __________
3. When did the customer buy it? __________
4. Where did the customer buy the product? __________
5. How much did the item cost? __________
6. What is the problem with the product? __________
7. When did the customer contact the store? __________

Example 2

Questions 1-10

Answer the following questions.

*Write **NO MORE THAN THREE WORDS** for each answer.*

1. What does Jane suggest doing at first? __________
2. What does Jack suggest instead? __________
3. Which part of town does Jack suggest they go to eat? __________
4. What kind of food does Jane like? __________
5. Why is Jack not keen on that food? __________
6. What is the name of the restaurant they decide to go to? __________
7. What time are they going to meet? __________
8. Where are they going to meet? __________
9. What's the telephone number of the restaurant? __________
10. How many people does the restaurant hold? __________

Example 3

Questions 1-5

Answer the following questions.

*Write **NO MORE THAN THREE WORDS** for each answer.*

1. What else has Brain been spending his time on except being with family? __________
2. What is the name of the scheme Brain is on? __________
3. What is the feature of this trial scheme? __________
4. How can Brain keep himself updated? __________
5. Does Brain pay income tax? __________

4周攻克

雅思听力周计划

第三周　常考场景精练

第三周	场景练习
星期一	租房：电话找房，向朋友咨询租房；与房东谈论租房
星期二	学校：语言学习；课程咨询；图书馆预约书
星期三	旅行：与朋友谈论度假计划；导游介绍伦敦塔轶事；旅游公司合作
星期四	健康和医疗：牙齿健康调查；节食；中西医
星期五	生活：讨论生日聚会；有机牛排；看朋友的孩子
星期六	环保：回收电池；保护宠物免受野生动物攻击；温室效应
星期日	科研：讨论科研；论文写作；申请项目基金

星期一

租房

本日主要学习租房，包括电话找房，向朋友咨询租房，与房东谈论租房。

场景一：电话找房

Questions 1-3

Fill the following blanks.

*Write **NO MORE THAN THREE WORDS** for each answer.*

❶ The apartment is on the ____________ floor.

❷ It is about ten minutes walk from the ____________ close to the Bath University.

❸ The man keeps a pet ____________ .

Questions 4-8

*Choose the correct letter **A**, **B** or **C**.*

❹ Which room is rather small?

A. kitchen B. washroom C. living room

❺ What is available?

A. internet access B. wardrobes C. microwave oven

❻ What is not included in the rent?

A. water and electricity B. heating C. maintenance

❼ How long would the contract be for?

A. one year B. two years C. no limit

❽ Why does the owner want to rent the place out?

A. Because he is going to buy another house.

B. Because he thinks it's too big.

C. Because he will not be using it.

Questions 9-10

Fill the following blanks.

*Write **NO MORE THAN THREE WORDS** for each answer.*

❾ The landlady is going to work at ____________ university.

❿ Her address is ____________ .

场景二：向朋友咨询租房

Questions 1-3

*Choose the correct letter **A**, **B** or **C**.*

❶ Who is Shirley?

A. Mohamod's former professor

B. somebody Mohamod knew before

C. Mohamod's close friend

❷ What is Shirley going to do for Mohamod?

A. She is going to help him to rent an apartment.

B. She will let Mohamod live in her apartment.

C. She will not do anything specific for him.

❸ To rent an apartment in New York is

A. easy. B. not mentioned. C. difficult.

Questions 4-5

Fill the following blanks.

*Write **NO MORE THAN THREE WORDS** for each answer.*

❹ Shirley suggests him to rent an apartment on ____________ .

❺ Mohamod will probably have to pay for about ____________ .

Question 6

*Choose the correct letter **A**, **B** or **C**.*

❻ Who is going to pay for him?

A. His parents. B. Himself. C. His company.

场景三：与房东谈论租房

Questions 1-2

Fill the following blanks.

*Write **NO MORE THAN THREE WORDS** for each answer.*

❶ George wants to have the locks ____________ .

❷ The lock problem will be solved in at most ____________ .

Questions 3-8

*Choose the correct answer **A**, **B** or **C**.*

❸ The problem with the kitchen is

A. no windows.

B. taps are leaking.

C. the sink is not very good.

❹ What will be done to the problems in kitchen?

A. The landlord will help soon.

B. The superintendent will come to fix it the next date.

C. George will have to ask for help.

❺ How is the paint?

A. It is pretty dingy.

B. It is smelly.

C. It is new.

❻ If George paints himself ,

A. he will have to pay by himself.

B. the landlord will give him the money.

C. they will share the price.

❼ What is not included in the rules?

A. No pets. B. No music. C. No noise.

❽ If George decides to rent, he will have to pay

A. $ 860 altogether including gas and water.

B. twelve-month rent altogether.

C. a month's deposit and a month's rent.

星期二 学校

本日主要学习内容是学校常见的场景，包括语言学习；课程咨询；图书馆预约书。

场景一：语言学习

Complete the blanks in the table below.
Write ***NO MORE THAN THREE WORDS*** *for each answer.*

spend the time	Spending time enjoyably ❶ ____________ the language
listen and read every day	One hour of listening or reading is ❷ ____________ than many hours of class time.
focus on ❸ ____________	Learn them through your listening and reading
❹ ______________ for your own learning	A teacher cannot teach you to become fluent
relax and enjoy yourself	That is the greatest ❺ __________ of success

场景二：课程咨询

Questions 1-3

Choose the correct answer ***A, B*** *or* ***C.***

❶ The caller has to learn a foreign language because

A. the caller is interested in foreign language learning.

B. the caller's school requires so.

C. the caller wants to use the foreign language in computer learning.

❷ They provide the following courses except.

A. French **B.** Spanish **C.** Chinese **D.** Japanese

❸ How much will the caller pay if he books two courses?

A. £25 **B.** £50 **C.** about £38

Questions 4-5

Answer the following questions.

Write ***NO MORE THAN THREE WORDS*** *for each answer.*

❹ The extension the caller should call is ______ .

❺ The computer classes meet on ________________ .

Question 6

Choose the correct letter ***A, B*** *or* ***C.***

❻ Which computer course is the most expensive one?

A. Word **B.** Excel **C.** PowerPoint

场景三：图书馆预约书

Questions 1-4

Answer the following questions.

Write ***NO MORE THAN THREE WORDS*** *for each answer.*

❶ The customer's name is ______ .

❷ The customer cannot reserve a book immediately because of his ______ .

❸ The customer's address is ______ .

❹ The customer's home number is ______ .

Questions 5-6

Choose the correct letter ***A, B*** *or* ***C.***

❺ The customer want to reserve a book under the category of

A. Psychology.

B. Sociology.

C. Anthropology.

❻ When will the customer collect the book?

A. Thursday afternoon

B. Friday morning

C. Friday afternoon

星期三

旅　行

今天我们学习旅行场景，主要内容包括与朋友谈论度假计划、导游介绍伦敦塔轶事。

场景一：与朋友谈论度假计划

Question 1

Answer the following question.

Write ***NO MORE THAN THREE WORDS*** *for it.*

❶ Bob wants the holiday because he ______ .

Questions 2-5

Choose the correct letter ***A, B*** *or* ***C.***

❷ This morning, Brain

A. called the travel agent.

B. visited the travel agent.

C. asked the travel agent to send him some brochures.

❸ Why don't they want to go abroad?

A. Because they cannot afford that.

B. Because they do not like other countries.

C. Because they do not have enough time.

❹ Where is more adventurous?

A. The South of Wales　B. Northern Ireland　C. Scotland

❺ Which is the cheapest?

A. The South of Wales　B. Northern Ireland　C. Scotland

Question 6

Answer the following question.

Write ***NO MORE THAN THREE WORDS*** *for each answer.*

❻ They decide to live in ______hotel.

Question 7

Choose the correct letter ***A, B*** *or* ***C.***

❼ Which is true about the breakfast in the hotel?

A. It's free.

B. They need pay a small amount of money to get in.

C. It's 10 for two guests.

Question 8

*Choose two letters from **A**, **B**, **C**, **D** or **E** to answer the following question.*

❽ Choose two facilities that are available in the hotel.

A. gymnasium B. tennis court C. massage service

D. sauna E. indoor swimming pool

场景二：导游介绍伦敦塔轶事

Questions 1-3

Answer the following questions.

*Write **NO MORE THAN THREE WORDS** for each answer.*

❶ The Tower of London was built by ______ .

❷ The Tower of London was a place of ______ .

❸ The heads of criminals were left on London Bridge to warn the ______ .

Question 4

*Choose the correct letter **A**, **B** or **C**.*

❹ Where had the two princes gone?

A. They were killed.

B. They escaped.

C. They stayed in the Tower of London.

Question 5

Answer the following question.

*Write **NO MORE THAN THREE WORDS** for each answer.*

❺ The princes were eventually buried in ______ .

Question 6

*Choose the correct letter **A**, **B** or **C**.*

❻ Guy Fawkes

A. blew up the parliament in 1605.

B. suffered terribly before his death.

C. invented the torturous rack.

场景三：旅游公司合作

Questions 1-2

Answer the following questions.

*Write **NO MORE THAN THREE WORDS** for each answer.*

❶ The time in London is ______________________________.

❷ There will be ________________ people in each group.

Questions 3-5

*Choose the correct letter, **A**, **B** or **C**.*

❸ What is the price for an adult on a weekday tour?

A. 89 pounds **B.** 99 pounds **C.** 49 pounds

❹ How long does the whole experience take?

A. one hour **B.** two hours **C.** four hours

❺ Can tourist have photographic record of the climb?

A. No, because they are not allowed to take cameras.

B. Yes, they can have photos from professional photographers.

C. No, they are not allowed to take pictures.

星期四

健康和医疗

今天的学习内容是健康和医疗，包括牙齿健康调查；节食；中西医。

场景一：牙齿健康调查

Questions 1-4

*Choose the correct letter **A**, **B** or **C**.*

❶ The respondent brushes his teeth

A. three times a day.

B. once a day.

C. more than three times a day.

❷ At what time doesn't the respondent brush his teeth?

A. before his meal

B. before go to bed

C. before work

❸ Which of the following is not true about the herbal toothpaste the respondent uses?

A. It is fluoride free.

B. It is cheaper than ordinary toothpaste.

C. It smells not very good.

❹ The respondent will take time off work to go to the dentist

A. very often.

B. only when he couldn't make an appointment with the dentist.

C. never.

Question 5

Answer the following question.

*Write **NO MORE THAN THREE WORDS** for each answer.*

❺ It takes about ______ to visit a dentist.

Questions 6-7

*Choose the correct letter **A**, **B** or **C**.*

❻ Compared to five years ago,

A. he visits the dentist more often now.

B. he visits the dentist less now.

C. it's about the same frequency of visiting dentist.

❼ Generally speaking, the respondent's attitude to dentists is

A. rather positive.

B. neutral.

C. rather negative.

场景二：节食

Questions 1-4

Answer the following questions.

Write ***NO MORE THAN THREE WORDS*** *for each answer.*

❶ The general purpose of dieting is to ______ .

❷ The right dieting concept should be keeping ______ .

❸ Fast foods have ______ .

❹ Rice is high in ______ .

Questions 5-8

Choose the correct letter ***A, B*** *or* ***C***.

❺ What is true about meat?

A. Meat is full of protein, so it is healthy, people can eat as much as they like.

B. Red meat is better, so it is more expensive.

C. White meat is healthier and it's cheaper than red meat.

❻ What is not true about fish?

A. Fish is a very healthy food.

B. Steamed fish is good.

C. Eating fish may lead to overweight.

❼ What is true about bread?

A. Bread may make people fat.

B. White bread is healthier than brown bread.

C. Bread is very healthy food, people can eat as much as they like.

❽ Which of the following is true?

A. Among three meals a day, one can eat some sweets.

B. Medium size meals are healthier.

C. Yoghurt is good to eat with three meals.

场景三：中西医

Questions 1-4

Answer the following questions.

Write ***NO MORE THAN THREE WORDS*** *for each answer.*

❶ Joy is going to specialize in ______ .

❷ The Chinese medicine places more emphasis on ______ .

❸ Western medicine tends to diagnose and treat specific ______ .

❹ The painkiller may kill the pain but not the ______ .

Questions 5-6

*Choose the correct letter **A**, **B** or **C**.*

❺ What is right about acupuncture?

A. Some people get it even when they are healthy.

B. Acupuncture hurts.

C. The purpose of acupuncture is to stop the energy channels.

❻ What disease can't be cured by acupuncture?

A. drug addiction

B. high blood pressure

C. none

星期五

生活

本日话题为生活，包括讨论生日聚会；有机牛排；看朋友的孩子。

场景一：讨论生日聚会

Questions 1-2

Answer the following questions.

*Write **NO MORE THAN THREE WORDS** for each answer.*

❶ Sarah's birthday is on next ______ .

❷ Sarah was thinking of having a ______ .

Questions 3-7

*Choose the correct letter **A, B** or **C**.*

❸ Where would Sarah hold the party?

A. in a hired room **B.** in her own room **C.** in Sue's room

❹ What type of food would they order?

A. Italian **B.** Japanese **C.** Thai

❺ What kind of music would they listen to?

A. dance music **B.** classical **C.** jazz

❻ They are not going to drink

A. beer. **B.** wine. **C.** spirits.

❼ When would they start the party?

A. 6:00 **B.** 7:00 **C.** 7:30

场景二：有机牛排

Questions 1-3

*Choose the correct letter **A, B** or **C**.*

❶ Johnson

A. is a vegetarian. **B.** likes eating all kinds of meat. **C.** only eat organic food.

❷ Organic beef comes from

A. any ox that ate cereal.

B. ox that is fed in the traditional way.

C. genetically modified ox.

❸ If the newspapers found a company was deliberately selling an unsafe product,

A. the company would go into bankruptcy soon.

B. the company would rise their share price.

C. the company would have a lot of business.

Question 4

Answer the following question.

*Write **NO MORE THAN THREE WORDS** for it.*

❹ Sales of organic food in supermarkets have risen by

A. 35%.　　B. 1%.　　C. 20%.

Questions 5-6

*Choose the correct letter **A, B** or **C**.*

❺ What animal diseases might be caused by genetically modified food?

A. Sheep's foot and mouth disease.

B. Egg flu.

C. Cows' foot and mouth disease.

场景三：看朋友的孩子

Questions 1-5

Answer the following questions.

*Write **NO MORE THAN THREE WORDS** for each answer.*

❶ Susan's baby was born on ______ .

❷ The baby will be called ______ .

❸ The baby weighed about ______ .

❹ The baby has ______ hair.

❺ Susan lives at ______ .

Questions 6-7

*Choose the correct letter **A, B** or **C**.*

❻ What do they plan to take?

A. They will take some flowers.

B. They will take a toy for the baby.

C. It is not decided yet.

❼ How would the wife go the second day?

A. Her husband will pick her up at home.

B. Her husband will pick her up at the supermarket.

C. She would go to the hospital by herself.

星期六

环保

今天场景为环保，包括回收电池；保护宠物免受野生动物攻击；温室效应。

场景一：回收电池

Questions 1-5

Answer the following questions.

*Write **NO MORE THAN THREE WORDS** for each answer.*

❶ The average American discards ______ each year.

❷ The metals found in batteries include mercury, cadmium, lead and ______ .

❸ ______ batteries contain lead and acid.

❹ ______ batteries have reduced the amount of batteries that need to be recycled.

❺ Wet-cell batteries are typically found in cars, boats and ______ .

场景二：保护宠物免受野生动物攻击

Question 1

*Choose **A, B** or **C.***

❶ What do coyotes look like?

A. They look like big wolves.

B. They look like dogs.

C. They look like cats.

Questions 2-6

Fill the following blanks.

*Write **NO MORE THAN THREE WORDS** for each answer.*

preventative measures	
Install a wooden fence	at least 2 ______ feet tall
Supervise your pet 3 ______	Walk your dog for nightly potty breaks before dark
Make noise on walks	loud noises will 4 ______ a coyote
Never leave 5 ______ outside	food can invite unwanted wildlife to your yard
Neuter your dog	coyotes can mate with unaltered 6 ______
Pick fruit off trees	pick the fruit so as not to entice coyotes to your property

场景三：温室效应

Questions 1-7

Complete the following sentences.

Write ***NO MORE THAN THREE WORDS*** *for each answer.*

❶ Global warming is caused by too much ______ .

❷ Greenhouse gasses can only absorb infrared radiation within narrow______ .

❸ As the concentration of CO_2 increases, there is______ infrared radiation in its spectrum to absorb.

❹ In some cases, the absorption spectra of Carbon Dioxide and Water Vapor______ .

❺ Humans have no control over the concentration of______ in the atmosphere.

❻ Water Vapor is ______ contributor to the overall greenhouse effect.

❼ When water vapor______ is low, CO_2 absorbs more of the radiation.

星期日 科研

今天的场景是科研，包括讨论科研；论文写作；申请项目基金。

场景一：讨论科研

Questions 1-6

Listen and fill the table below.

Write ***NO MORE THAN THREE WORDS*** *for each answer.*

type of media		how we can use each medium
the 1 ______ media	books and magazine	ideal for students to use 2 ______
audio forms of media	CDs and 3 ______	small group of students
4 ______ media	film, television and videos	ideal for use with 5 ______
6 ______ media	computers	Not useful with a whole class

场景二：论文写作

Questions 1-2

Listen and complete the summary below.

Write ***NO MORE THAN THREE WORDS*** *for each answer.*

The purpose of an introduction is to __1__ your readers to your paper and get their __2__ from the beginning.

It's essential that you get the introduction right. This means that you must know what the introduction is supposed to do, what sorts of things must go into the introduction, how to write and structure the introduction properly, and how to interest your reader from the start.

An introduction should do the following:

Questions 3-12

Complete the following sentences.

Write ***NO MORE THAN THREE WORDS*** *for each answer.*

- □ __3__ a reader's interest
- □ indicate the __4__ and direction of the paper, and act as a navigation guide to its reading
- □ show the reader how you are __5__ the question

- provide a __6__ for the main issue
- indicate the __7__ of the paper
- indicate your __8__ and point of view

The question of the example introduction is what communication problems might arise in a __9__ , and how can managers best deal with them?

In the introduction, the writer mentioned that over the past twenty five years, Australia embraced __10__ as a policy, so issues of intercultural communication have become more and more prominent in the workplace.

However, little had been written on these issues, and many organizational managers have no training or knowledge of how to deal with communication problems, even though most workplaces are staffed by people of __11__. An ignorance of the different forms of __12__ used by other cultures can lead to misunderstandings and unpleasantness.

场景三：申请项目基金

Questions 1-3

*Choose the correct letter **A, B** or **C**.*

❶ How many people are there in the research team?

A. 2 **B.** 3 **C.** 4

❷ The research team is interested in investigating problems with

A. reading habits. **B.** watching TV. **C.** learning with parents.

❸ According to the survey, how many hours average readers spend on watching TV?

A. 2 **B.** 5 **C.** 10

Question 4

Answer the following question.

*Write **NO MORE THAN THREE WORDS** for it.*

❹ If children spend less time on TV, they will automatically spend more time learning with _____ .

Questions 5-7

*Choose the correct letter **A, B** or **C**.*

❺ How many parents are they going to interview?

A. 8 **B.** 50 **C.** 150

❻ How much grant is the research group applying for?

A. 1000 **B.** 1500 **C.** 3300

❼ Who is likely to get the most benefit from the research?

A. parents **B.** pupils **C.** teachers

4周攻克

雅思听力周计划

第四周　七天模拟，强力冲刺

第四周	Model Test	Section 1	Section 2	Section 3	Section 4
星期一	Model Test 1	找工作	赴澳准备	完成作业	自行车发展史
星期二	Model Test 2	雅思报名	失眠	介绍大学	琥珀
星期三	Model Test 3	讨论童年	防止汽车被盗	收音机	东伦敦历史
星期四	Model Test 4	保险	节日安排	讨论报告	高等教育
星期五	Model Test 5	顾客咨询	体育运动	语言学习评估	水资源
星期六	Model Test 6	租车	购物习惯	温室效应	化妆品研究
星期日	Model Test 7	签证	退休金	讨论学位申请	讲座介绍

星期一

Model Test 1

雅思试卷样式

Candidate Number

Candidate Name ______________________

INTERNATIONAL ENGLISH LANGUAGE TESTING SYSTEM **0380/4**
0381/4

Listening

PRACTICE MATERIALS Approximately 30 minutes

Additional materials:
Answer sheet for Listening and Reading

Time Approximately 30 minutes (plus 10 minutes' transfer time)

INSTRUCTIONS TO CANDIDATES

Do not open this question paper until you are told to do so.

Write your name and candidate number in the spaces at the top of this page.

Listen to the instructions for each part of the paper carefully.

Answer all the questions.

While you are listening, write your answers on the question paper.

You will have 10 minutes at the end of the test to copy your answers onto the separate answer sheet. Use a pencil.

At the end of the test, hand in this question paper.

INFORMATION FOR CANDIDATES

There are **four** parts to the test.

You will hear each part **once** only.

There are **40** questions.

Each question carries one mark.

For each part of the test, there will be time for you to look through the questions and time for you to check your answers.

SECTION 1 *Questions 1–10*

Questions 1-6

Complete the notes below.

Write **NO MORE THAN THREE WORDS** *for each answer.*

Example answer

The interviewee's address: 32 Acacia Avenue.

1. The interviewee's postcode: __________.
2. It is the __________ year for the interviewee in the vnirersity.
3. The interviewee's major: __________.

Working experiences	Reason to quit
In a flower shop	4. ________
5. ________	It took too much time.
6. ________	She wants to get some experience in her major.

Questions 7-10

Fill the blank with **A, B,** *or* **C**. **A** *refers to no problem,* **B** *means possible,* **C** *means not OK.*

Weekends	7. ________
Evenings	8. ________
Holidays	9. ________
Lunch time	10. ________

SECTION 2 *Questions 11-20*

Questions 11-14

Complete the sentences below.

Write **NO MORE THAN THREE WORDS** *for each answer.*

11. Australia has become a popular place for people to go for further education __________.
12. The education system in Australia is very __________.
13. Students can gain the right balance of __________and __________.
14. The Australian Qualifications Framework (AQF) is a __________ system.

Questions 15-17

Choose the correct letter, **A**, **B** *or* **C**.

15. The universities in Australia are
    A. mainly private.
    B. mainly public.
    C. half private and have public.
16. In Australia, students can enjoy the following except
    A. advanced teaching facilities.

B. professional lecturers.

C. free education.

17. Australia is regarded as a harmonious nation, because there is no

A. crime.　　B. war.　　C. religion.

Questions 18-20

Complete the table below.

*Write **NO MORE THAN THREE WORDS** for each answer.*

Australian citizens come from	18 __________ countries
19 __________ of its people	Were born in another country
20 __________ of its population	Speak other language at home

SECTION 3 *Questions 21-30*

Questions 21-23

Complete the notes below.

*Write **NO MORE THAN THREE WORDS** for each answer.*

21. George's essay is about __________.

22. Generally speaking, the professor is __________ with George's writing.

23. George gets some statistics from __________.

Questions 24-26

*Choose the correct letter, **A**, **B** or **C**.*

24. What is the problem with his introduction?

A. The lead-in is not very clear.

B. He needs more background information.

C. He has too much background information.

25. What is the problem with the literature review?

A. He has no literature review.

B. He should review more.

C. He need reorganize his literature review.

26. What's the problem with data presentation?

A. The data is not sufficient.

B. The figures are too straightforward.

C. Some visual tools should be applied.

Questions 27-30

Complete the sentences below

*Write **NO MORE THAN THREE WORDS** for each answer.*

27. Brian is good at __________.

28. There should be a __________ paragraph before his conclusion.
29. George worried about the __________ of his essay if he hasn't drawn an early conclusion.
30. George is supposed to hand in his revised version __________.

SECTION 4 *Questions 31-40*

Questions 31-32

*Choose the correct letter, **A**, **B** or **C**.*

31. The term bicycle was coined
    A. in the 1860s.
    B. in the early 19th century.
    C. in 1817.
32. The first mechanically-driven bicycle was believed to have been built in
    A. Germany. **B.** Scotland. **C.** France.

Questions 33-36

Complete the sentences below.
*Write **NO MORE THAN THREE WORDS** for each answer.*

33. The first really popular and commercially successful design was developed around __________.
34. That the popularity of bicycles dropped off in USA between 1900 and 1910 is because ______ became the preferred means of transportation.
35. Only in the 1930s did European racing organizations allow racers to use __________.
36. When racers were allowed to use derailleurs, racing times immediately __________.

Questions 37-40

Complete the table below.
*Write **NO MORE THAN THREE WORDS** for each answer.*

two predominant bicycle styles for recreational cyclists in North America at Mid-century		
	Heavyweight cruiser bicycles	Lighter cycles
Tires	37 _________ tires	hand brakes
brakes	pedal-driven "coaster" brakes	38 _________ tires
gear	only one gear	39 _________ hub gearing system
Advantages	Durable, comfort, streamlined appearance, and a significant array of 40 ___________	Durable , comfortable, practical

周计划提示

答案速查见 P105　听力原文见 P169

星期二

Model Test 2

SECTION 1 *Questions 1-10*

Questions 1-5

Complete the notes below.

Write ***NO MORE THAN THREE WORDS*** *for each answer.*

1. The candidate needs to take the test on __________.
2. The speaking part of the test is often on __________.
3. The candidate needs to bring his ID, a copy of his ID and __________
4. According to the standard requirement from Cambridge, there is __________ breaks between different parts of the test.
5. It takes __________ for the result to be processed.

Questions 6-10

Complete the notes below.

Write ***NO MORE THAN THREE WORDS*** *for each answer.*

The examination fee is	HK$ __________
Pay by cash in	__________
The address	__________ Road, Hong Kong.
The post code	__________
Tel.	__________

SECTION 2 *Questions 11-20*

Insomnia is a symptom that can accompany sleep, medical and 11 __________ disorder.

According to the United States Department of Health and Human Services in the year 2007, approximately 12 __________ Americans regularly suffer from insomnia each year.

Insomnia types	Duration	Causes	Consequences
Chronic	less than a week	13 __________, changes in the sleep environment, the timing of sleep, severe depression, or stress	sleepiness and impaired psychomotor performance
Acute	less than 14 __________		unable to consistently sleep well for a period of time
Transient	longer than a month	a primary disorder	unable to sleep, 15 __________ fatigue, hallucinations, and/or mental fatigue

16. Who had the lowest rates of mortality?

A. Those who sleep for fewer than 6 hours.

B. Those who sleep for more than 8 hours.

C. Those who sleep for 7 hours.

17. Which of the following situation would not increased the mortality rate by 15%?
    A. Getting 8.5 or more hours of sleep per night.
    B. Those who get less than 3.5 hours sleep per night.
    C. Men who sleep less than 4.5 hours per night.
18. After controlling for sleep duration and insomnia, use of __________ was also found to be associated with an increased mortality rate.
19. To moderate insomnia for most people is associated with increased __________ .
20. Attention to __________ is an important first line treatment strategy.

SECTION 3 *Questions 21-30*

Questions 21-25

*Choose the correct letter, **A**, **B** or **C**.*

21. The University was founded in
    A. 1096.
    B. 1167.
    C. not known.
22. The first known overseas student is
    A. Gerald of Wales.
    B. Emo of Friesland.
    C. scolarum Oxonie.
23. The reason for the establishment of primitive halls of residence is
    A. the students fight with the people in the town.
    B. to resist the invading of outsiders.
    C. to disallow the students to go out of the university.
24. Popes and kings praise the university because of the following reasons except
    A. its curriculum.
    B. its doctrine.
    C. its famous professors.
25. What happened in 1530?
    A. Henry VIII was forced to divorce.
    B. Henry VIII forced the University to accept his divorce.
    C. Catherine of Aragon was forced to divorce by the university.

Questions 26-30

Complete the notes below.

*Write **NO MORE THAN THREE WORDS** for each answer.*

26. In the late 17th century, John Locke was forced to flee the country because he was suspected of __________.
27. The 18th century was an era of __________.

28. The University assumed a leading role in religious controversy in __________.

29. In 1860 the __________ was the site of a famous debate between Thomas Huxley and Bishop Wilberforce.

30. From __________, academic halls were established for women.

SECTION 4 *Questions 31-40*

31. What is amber?

    A. It is tree sap.

    B. It is fossilized resin.

    C. It is a stone.

32. The formation of amber takes __________.

33. The resin is produced to __________.

34. It floats in salt water because of its __________.

35. Wet sediments of clay and sand preserve the resin well because they are devoid of __________.

36. In ancient time, amber had been used for the following purposes, except

    A. medical purposes.

    B. ornament purposes.

    C. to make smoke and alcohol.

37. Now, amber can be used to cure many diseases when it is combined with __________.

38. Amber's place in culture and tradition has __________ value.

39. How many ambers can be recognized as good ones among 100,000 ambers?

    A. 10

    B. 100

    C. 1,000

40. The most highly-prized amber is __________.

周计划提示

答案速查见 P106　听力原文见 P176

星期三

Model Test 3

SECTION 1 *Questions 1-10*

Questions 1-4

Fill the following blanks.

Write ***NO MORE THAN THREE WORDS*** *for each answer.*

1. The girl's nationality: __________
2. The boy lives in __________, England.
3. The girl has __________ brothers.
4. The boy's childhood house was surrounded by __________

Questions 5-10

Choose the correct letter ***A, B*** *or* ***C****.*

5. Where did the girl's cousin often play football?
   A. In the football pitches.
   B. On grass land.
   C. On the playground.
6. Who doesn't like gardening?
   A. the girl　　**B.** the girl's mother　　**C.** the boy
7. What did the children in their childhood?
   A. playing computer games
   B. watching films
   C. chasing around with friends
   D. shooting the birds
   E. staying indoors
8. What's their parents' attitude to them when they were children?
   A. Do not care about their safety.
   B. Very nervous if they went out.
   C. Gave them freedom to have fun.
9. Which is true according to the listening materials?
   A. China is the safest place.
   B. It is too dangerous to bring up children in UK.
   C. Both China and UK are safe to live in.

10. Which of the following is not a reason for Vivian to love UK?
   A. It is very clean.
   B. People are very friendly.
   C. She loves the scenery there.

SECTION 2 *Questions 11-20*

Questions 11-15

*Choose the correct letter **A**, **B** or **C**.*

11. How many cars are stolen in this country?
   A. one car every 32 seconds
   B. a million cars so far
   C. 40 percent

12-13. What are the two places that are dangerous for cars?
   A. houses **B.** the garage **C.** working areas
   D. shopping centers **E.** sports center

14. How many drivers left their keys in the car and got their cars stolen?
   A. one in five **B.** five percent **C.** 40 percent

15. Who steals cars?
   A. joyriders **B.** professional drivers **C.** robberies

Questions 16 - 20

Complete the sentences.
*Write **NO MORE THAN THREE WORDS** for each answer.*

16. If your car breaks down, __________ before you go for help.
17. Dusk to __________ are the peak hours for car theft.
18. Park in a __________, preferably where there are plenty of passers-by.
19. Keep your __________ in your wallet or purse.
20. Have a record of your car's __________.

SECTION 3 *Questions 21-30*

Questions 21-25

Complete the following sentences.
*Write **NO MORE THAN THREE WORDS** for each answer.*

21. Broadcasting represents a critical national resource for __________.
22. All nations regulate broadcasting within their __________.
23. Many nations operate their own broadcasting systems through a __________.

*choose the correct letter **A**, **B** or **C**.*

24. If the broadcasting represents an independent voice, where would it get economic support?

A. tax revenues

B. profits by selling advertising time

C. permit a mixed system of commercial and publicly supported stations

25. What is true about the American broadcasting?

A. Most American stations are listener supported.

B. 10 percent of American broadcasting is non-commercial.

C. Most American stations get fund from the government.

Questions 26-27

Complete the following sentences.

Write ***NO MORE THAN THREE WORDS*** *for each answer.*

26. __________ of the households has a television.

27. In average, people listen to radio in America for more than __________ a day.

Questions 28-30

Choose the correct letter ***A, B*** *or* ***C****.*

28. Which is not true about American people and broadcasting?

A. American people like to listen to the president's speech.

B. Americans use broadcasting a lot for advertising.

C. There are many people in America listening to radios.

29. Which of the following is less likely to dominate the broadcast programming?

A. news

B. occasional educational shows

C. popular entertainers

30. What can be learnt about Rose?

A. Rose is going to the broadcast station.

B. Rose is going to buy a radio.

C. Rose is going to do a similar presentation.

SECTION 4 *Questions 31-40*

Questions 31-35

Complete the following sentences.

Write ***NO MORE THAN THREE WORDS*** *for each answer.*

31. Many people's conception about where East London is __________.

32. To the west, the border is the __________.

33. 500 years ago, the East End was just __________.

34. London's reputedly oldest riverside pub opened in __________.

35. The Norman St. Paul's Cathedral, which was some 180 feet __________ than the present one.

Questions 36-40

*Choose the correct letter **A**, **B** or **C**.*

36. In the 1600s,
    - **A.** the east side of London was a place for the rich people.
    - **B.** the west winds could blow the smells away.
    - **C.** the west end was very dirty and smelly.
37. In the Second World War,
    - **A.** the docks were destroyed.
    - **B.** Victorian London was safe.
    - **C.** London was not really influenced.
38. In 1969,
    - **A.** the Kray twins controlled the west end.
    - **B.** there was a war between the feudal lords and Kray twins.
    - **C.** there were many people out of work.
39. Since the 1980s,
    - **A.** East End of London start to boom again.
    - **B.** East End of London was a financial center.
    - **C.** financial crisis emerged.
40. It can be implied that
    - **A.** the government would provide East London with a lot of money.
    - **B.** government paid no attention to East London.
    - **C.** the future of East London could be optimistic.

周计划提示

答案速查见 P106　听力原文见 P182

星期四

Model Test 4

SECTION 1 *Questions 1-10*

Questions 1-5

Complete the table below.

Write ***NO MORE THAN THREE WORDS*** *for each answer.*

1. Name	
2. Birthday	
3. Address	
4. Policy number	
5. Time of the accident	

Questions 6-8

Choose ***A****,* ***B****, or* ***C****.*

6. In order to prove the accident, the customer has to provide

   A. supporting evidence.

   B. someone that witnessed the accdent.

   C. a statement given by a witness.

7. What is right with the policeman?

   A. The policeman did not know.

   B. The policeman came but did nothing.

   C. The policemen did the necessary thing.

8. How is the customer?

   A. The customer is terribly injured.

   B. The customer is slightly injured.

   C. The customer is in the hospital.

Questions 9-10

Fill the following blanks.

Write ***NO MORE THAN THREE WORDS*** *for eaeh answer.*

9. The customer is suggested to get checked in __________.

10. The accident happened in __________.

SECTION 2 *Questions 11-20*

Complete the sentences below.

Write ***NO MORE THAN THREE WORDS*** *for each answer.*

11. Before an holiday, one should compare the __________ he or she wants with the choices they can make.
12. Finding the best location to go __________ might take a bit of research.
13. You also need to think about what type of __________ you would like to stay in.

14-15. If you are going on an active holiday then you might like to opt for a hotel that has__________ and _________.

16. If you are visiting Goa you could have an authentic experience staying in their __________.
17. Some people will book a trip to a particular location with influence of their __________.
18. Local travel agent may provide some information in __________.
19. The best way to find one's ideal holiday is to __________.
20. If you want the height of luxury, you should go to stay in __________.

SECTION 3 *Questions 21-30*

Questions 21-23

Choose ***A****,* ***B*** *or* ***C****.*

21. What was wrong with Bob?

    A. He got a flu. **B.** He got an eye infection. **C.** He has eaten some bad food.

22. What are they going to do?

    A. They are going to do a project together.

    B. They are going to the hospital.

    C. They are going to the library.

23. Who will be in the same research group?

    A. Bob and Cathy **B.** Bob and Mr. Speary **C.** Cathy and Mr. Speary

Questions 24-27

Complete the notes below.

Write ***NO MORE THAN THREE WORDS*** *for each answer.*

24. The project is mainly __________.
25. The aim of the research is to find out the changes on __________.
26. Bob will get some information through __________.
27. Bob will focus on ____________________ for literature.

Questions 28-30

Choose ***A****,* ***B****, or* ***C****.*

28. What may they possibly look at?

    A. bread and wine **B.** dresses **C.** mp3

29. How will Cathy help Bob with his notes?

A. She will copy for him.
B. She have had a copy for him.
C. She will give him the notes latter.

30. When will they meet again?
A. They will have lunch together.
B. They will have dinner together.
C. They will meet the next day.

SECTION 4 *Questions 31-40*

Questions 31-33

Complete the sentences below.

*Write **NO MORE THAN THREE WORDS** for each answer.*

31. Higher education is different from other forms of education because of the level of intellectual difficulty associated with its curriculum and curriculum is concerned with _________ problems.
32. The main aim of higher education is to enable society to ___________ through an understanding of itself and its world.
33. Traditionally, higher education is regarded as an academic community enquiring into problems for __________.

Questions 34-35

*Choose **A, B** or **C**.*

34. What is the government's attitude towards higher education?
A. Higher education should be academic communities only.
B. The government denied the traditional function of higher education.
C. Higher education should have new functions.

35. What has not been mentioned?
A. Equipping the labour force with the key transferable skills needed for employment.
B. Help the firms to be profitable.
C. Generating economic development.

Questions 36-40

*Fill the table. Write **NO MORE THAN THREE WORDS** for each answer.*

	Reasons for the professor to choose the topic
36	It is a good __________ of the professor's main theme.
37	It is the __________ between research, scholarship and teaching.
38	Unless there are benefits to teaching, there is no __________ case for doing research.
39	Expenditure levels on research are not yet __________.
40	The alleged link is the basis for statements about the __________ of some institutions or departments over others.

周计划提示

答案速查见 P107　听力原文见 P187

星期五

Model Test 5

SECTION 1 *Questions 1-10*

Questions 1-5

Complete the table below.

Write ***NO MORE THAN THREE WORDS*** *for each answer.*

Name	1
Reasons for calling	2
Destination	3
Address	4
Postcode	5

Questions 6-8

Choose ***A****,* ***B****, or* ***C****.*

6. What is the size of the box?

   A. It's 2.5m long, 1.5m wide and 1.75m deep.

   B. It's 2.5m long, 1.75m wide and 1.5m high.

   C. It's 2.5m long, 1.55m wide and 1.70m deep.

7. What can be inferred from what the agent said?

   A. Only books and clothes can be shipped in their company.

   B. Anything that is easy to break cannot be shipped.

   C. They can ship anything except wine and perfume.

8. How would the caller deal with the wine and perfume?

   A. It is not mentioned.

   B. He will ship it.

   C. He will take it with him.

Questions 9-10

Complete the sentences below.

Write ***NO MORE THAN THREE WORDS*** *for each answer.*

9. The value of the clothes is __________.

10. The value of the total contents is __________.

SECTION 2 *Questions 11-20*

Question 11

Complete the sentence.

Write ***NO MORE THAN THREE WORDS*** *for it.*

11. Jogging is unique in that it combines some of the rigors and intensity of running and ________.

Questions 12-13

Choose two of the letters to answer the question.

12-13. Which benefits are not mentioned by the speaker?

A. increased functioning of the heart and lungs

B. increasing muscles

C. increasing joint mobility

D. losing weight

E. reducing stress

F. curing disease

Questions 14-15

Complete the sentences below.

Write ***NO MORE THAN THREE WORDS*** *for each answer.*

14. Before an exercises program, one is suggested to check the ________.

15. The very fit people would better start with ________.

Questions 16-20

Complete the table below.

Write ***NO MORE THAN THREE WORDS*** *for each answer.*

Preparation	A proper diet	three meals per day; includes all basic16. ________
	17. ________	jogging may requires 18. ________ per day of fluids, which includes water and electrolytes such as sodium, potassium, magnesium, and calcium.
Key equipment	Clothing	appropriate to the weather, layered for easy 19. ________ in cooler temperatures; absorbent is best
	shoes	fit, but also cushioning, 20. ________, stability, sole thickness, and arch support

SECTION 3 *Questions 21-30*

Questions 21-24

Complete the sentences below.

Write ***NO MORE THAN THREE WORDS*** *for each answer.*

21. Alex felt ________ on how his English was going on.

22. The professor suggested him to try some ________.

23. The first thing the example student did was to ________.

24. Alex felt difficult to keep diaries because he did not like writing down things that are ______.

25. Alex wrote diary after a ________ class.

Questions 26-28

*Choose **A**, **B**, or **C**.*

26. What is Alex's problem with reading?
    A. He cannot read quickly.
    B. Reading is tiring.
    C. The weather is hot.
27. What did Alex do to improve?
    A. He tried to read faster.
    B. He read newspaper.
    C. He asked the lecturer for some reading skills.
28. Which is the statement that Alex still has problem with?
    A. I can catch the main idea.
    B. I can catch almost every word.
    C. I can get the attitude of the speaker.

Questions 29-30

Complete the sentences below.

*Write **NO MORE THAN THREE WORDS** for each answer.*

29. Alex found the progress cards __________.
30. The professor said Alex needed to be __________.

SECTION 4 *Questions 31-40*

Complete the table below.

*Write **NO MORE THAN THREE WORDS** for each answer.*

factors that contribute to the water stress		
1	31 ________ growth	It is estimated that by 2050 there will be an additional 32 ________ people.
2	33 ____________ of business activity	Business activity ranging from industrialization to services such as tourism and 34 _____ continues to expand rapidly.
3	Rapid 35 ________	Small private wells and septic tanks that work well in low-density communities are not feasible within 36 ________ urban areas.
4	37 ________ change	Rising temperatures will increase 38 ________ and lead to increases in precipitation.
5	Water 39 ________	Many pollutants threaten water supplies, but the most widespread is the discharge of 40 ________ into natural waters.

周计划提示

答案速查见 P107　听力原文见 P193

星期六

Model Test 6

SECTION 1 *Questions 1-10*

Questions 1-3

Complete the notes below.

Write ***NO MORE THAN THREE WORDS*** *for each answer.*

1．Name: ___________

2．Address: ___________

3．Telephone number: ___________

Questions 4-7

choose ***A, B, C*** *or* ***D.***

4-5．The equipments that both Grade C and Grade D have

A．air conditioning. **B**．music equipment. **C**．tax. **D**．first aid kit.

6．When will the man return the car?

A．Saturday **B**．Sunday **C**．Monday

7．Why can the man get discount?

A．Because he is from a special company.

B．Because he has a membership of the cmpany.

C．Because he is an old customer.

Questions 8-10

complete the sentence.

Write ***NO MORE THAN THREE WORDS*** *for each answer.*

8-10．The company will also provide ___________, ___________ and ___________.

SECTION 2 *Questions 11-20*

Questions 11-15

Complete the table below.

Write ***NO MORE THAN THREE WORDS*** *for each answer.*

Reasons for shopping	
We shop because we are depressed.	It's called 11 _________.
We shop because we deserve it.	shopping is taken as a 12 _________
We shop to feel more in control.	cash or plastic in your hand gives you control over 13 _________ and human beings love to be in control
We shop to make a point.	shop to prove that no one can tell you 14 _________
We shop to escape.	Going through the mall is your 15 _________

Questions 16-17

*Choose **A**, **B** or **C**.*

16. Which is not mentioned in the reason for shopping to be someone else?

    A. We believe that new shoes will make life better.

    B. The iphone we buy makes us feel important.

    C. We want our friend to be jealous.

17. Which of the followings is right?

    A. Shopping is just for women.

    B. Men go shopping only for wmen.

    C. Shopping satisfies our urge to socialize.

Questions 18-20

Complete the sentences below.

*Write **NO MORE THAN THREE WORDS** for each answer.*

18. We shop to fool ourselves because we thought walking in the mall is ___________ .

19. We shop to build our ego because we love the attention salespeople give us and the way they ___________ .

20. The first step to overcoming a bad shopping habit is to discover ___________ of doing it.

SECTION 3 *Questions 21-30*

Questions 21-22

Complete the diagram below.

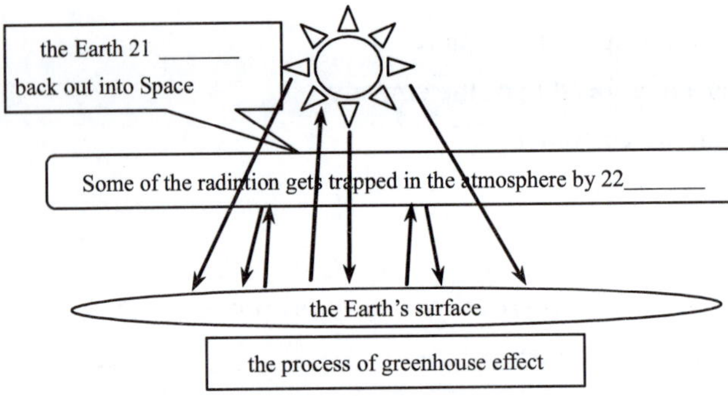

Questions 23-25

*Choose **A**, **B**, **C**,**D** or **E**.*

23-24. Which are not mentioned as resources of Methane?

   A. fields

   B. landfills

   C. rotten vegetation

   D. burning of fossil fuels

   E. dead body of animals

25. What city would not be submerged if ice caps keep melting?
 A. London B. New York C. Sydney D. Kyoto

Questions 26-30

Complete the following sentences.

Write ***NO MORE THAN THREE WORDS*** *for each answer.*

26. Optimistic scientists believe that positive feedbacks from ___________ and their water vapour could have an impact on global warming.
27. Skeptical scientists suspect that we have been wrong in our ___________ of the situation.
28. Without the Greenhouse Effect the planet would ___________.
29. When a volcano erupts it throws debris up into the stratosphere. This protects the earth from ___________.
30. ___________ take hundreds of years, which is slow enough for us to do something to prevent a catastrophe.

SECTION 4 *Questions 31-40*

31. Which of the following statements about cosmetics is not right?
 A. Cosmetics are colored products.
 B. Cosmetics are substances used to change people's appearance.
 C. Cosmetics could be substances used to change the odor of the human body.
32. The manufacture of cosmetics is dominated by a small number of ___________.
33. Evidence showed that the first usage of cosmetics is about ___________.
34. The Romans and Ancient Egyptians used cosmetics containing ___________.
35. In the Middle Ages cosmetics use was frowned upon by ___________.
36. A popular fad for women during the Middle Ages was to have a ___________ complexion.
37. Queen Victoria publicly declared makeup improper, vulgar, and acceptable only for use by ___________.
38. Women in the 19th century compared themselves to ___________.
39. The annual expenditures for cosmetics today are estimated at ___________.
40. L'Oréal was founded in ___________.

周计划提示

答案速查见 P108　听力原文见 P198

星期日

Model Test 7

SECTION 1 *Questions 1-10*

Questions 1-3

Complete the sentences below.

Write ***NO MORE THAN THREE WORDS*** *for each answer.*

1. One can hold ___________.
2. If one circumstances change you should always inform the ___________.
3. Visas for the UK can be issued only at ___________.

Questions 4-8

Choose ***A,B****, or* ***C****.*

4. Which is not mentioned as a reason for an application refused?
   A. Giving false or misleading information.
   B. Failing to give important relevant information on a visa application form.
   C. Failing to give money to an entry clearance officer.
5. Visa cannot be valid for
   A. 2 years. **B.** 4 years. **C.** 5 years. **D.** 10 years.
6. Which of the following is wrong for biometric data?
   A. All the people who apply for a visa need to provide biometric data.
   B. 10-digit finger scans and a digital photograph are taken for records.
   C. The applicant has to go in person to provide biometrics.
7. The finger scans are
   A. electronic. **B.** taken by using liquid. **C.** chemical.
8. Which of the following is OK?
   A. If your face got a hurt by a knife and it is recovering.
   B. You can take the photo with glasses.
   C. You cover your head for religious reasons.

Questions 9-10

Complete the sentences below.

Write ***NO MORE THAN THREE WORDS*** *for each answer.*

9. The biometrics data can be done in ___________.

10. If you are asked to attend an interview, you have to do this within __________ from the date the visa officer assesses your application.

SECTION 2 *Questions 11-20*

Questions 11-15

*Choose **A**, **B** or **C**.*

11. What are the three important ways to support one's retirement?
   A. pension, home and deposit accounts
   B. pension, home and investments
   C. pension, home and all other savings and invesiments
12. What is not a category of pension?
   A. state pensions **B.** insurance **C.** company schemes
13. What does tax relief mean?
   A. It means if you save in a pension, you do not have to pay tax.
   B. It means pension actually helps you to pay less tax.
   C. It means the taxman will increase your pension.
14. If you have an individual personal pension,
   A. your contributions will not be taxed before they go in to your fund.
   B. basic rate tax is the same no pension.
   C. higher rate taxpayers can claim back additional tax relief.
15. If you have a company pension,
   A. contributions are deducted from your gross salary before income tax.
   B. as income tax is based on your pay before deducting your contributions.
   C. you automatically receive tax relief at your lowest rate.

Questions 16-20

Fill the table bellow.
*Write **NO MORE THAN THREE WORDS** for each answer.*

benefits of using pensions to save for retirement		
1	tax relief	When you save in a pension the taxman helps to increase your pension pot by providing 16 ______ , subject to certain limits.
2	17 _______ growth	Money in your pension fund grows largely free of tax
3	Employer 18 _______	With company pensions your employer makes contributions to your pension, increasing the amount going into your fund.
4	Access to tax free cash in retirement	When you take your benefits you may have the option of taking up to 19 _______ of the pension fund you have built up as tax free cash.
5	Access to investing in funds	By saving in a pension, you're able to put your money in a range of 20 _______ .

SECTION 3 *Questions 21-30*

Questions 21-23

*Choose **A**, **B**, or **C**.*

21. Who can use the undergraduate degree application?
  A. All the undergraduates who have completed 80 credits.
  B. All the undergraduates who are earning an undergraduate certificate.
  C. All the undergraduates who have completed 90 credits and are earning an undergraduate certificate.
22. What if the student cannot get into the application system?
  A. The student has to check his or her total credits.
  B. The student has to check his or her total credits and make sure the paperwork has been processed.
  C. Go to log in the system at college office.
23. Which is not right about the graduation term?
  A. Students can apply for graduation one year ahead of their expected graduation date.
  B. If you don't see the term in which you want to graduate means the deadline have passed.
  C. If the student applies too early, he or she can not see the graduation term.

Questions 24-30

Complete the notes below.

*Write **NO MORE THAN THREE WORDS** for each answer.*

24. If the student missed the deadline to apply, he or she can select __________.
25. If the student choose to cancel and exit, he or she will __________.
26. If the student has two degrees to apply for, he or she would have to complete _______ application.
27. The applicant will be asked to __________ the application before submitting.
28. Changes can be made __________.
29. If the applicant wants the diploma to be sent to a third party, the address should be filled in the __________ .
30. One you hit "submit", the applicant can see a __________ screen.

SECTION 4 *Questions 31-40*

31. Which of the following is not right for the lectures in the University's Climate, Sustainability and Society lecture series?
  A. Speakers will draw on science perspectives to address the issues surrounding climate change and sustainability.
  B. Speakers will draw on social science perspectives to address the issues surrounding climate change and sustainability.
  C. Speakers will draw on political perspectives to address the issues surrounding climate

change and sustainability.

D. Speakers will draw on economic perspectives to address the issues surrounding climate change and sustainability.

32. How many people have listened to the first lecture given by Professor Barrie Bush?

A. 330

B. 120

C. 450

33. The second lecture commences on __________.

34. The third and final lecture of the series starts at __________.

35. Climate, Sustainability and Society is a __________ subject.

36. Which department hasn't participated in the development of the lecture series?

A. the faculties of Law and Management

B. the faculties of Science, Technology and Engineering

C. the Humanities and Social Science department

D. the faculties of Human and Society

37. The teaching will take a __________.

38. Students who complete the subject will be able to bring advanced decision making to __________.

39. Students enrolled in the subject will attend the lectures to gain an appreciation of the relationship between advocacy and __________.

40. These lectures will be __________.

周计划提示

答案速查见 P109　听力原文见 P204

附录1 练习答案

第一周 雅思听力基本功训练

第一周 星期三 练习听数字

基数词、序数词、分数、百分数、小数

（cardinal numbers, ordinal numbers, fractions, percentages, decimals）

练习1. Listen to some number and write them down in the table.

1.	15	2.	50	3.	55	4.	67
5.	48	6.	81	7.	80	8.	18
9.	19	10.	28	11.	35	12.	77
13.	90	14.	33	15.	64	16.	89
17.	105	18.	118	19.	115	20.	150
21.	222	22.	345	23.	565	24.	901
25.	999	26.	109	27.	119	28.	190
29.	808	30.	771	31.	442	32.	677
33.	9,000	34.	5,555	35.	1,002	36.	4,667
37.	8,030	38.	4,090	39.	1,234	40.	5,890
41.	7,112	42.	3,337	43.	2,334	44.	6,008
45.	6,006	46.	2,111	47.	3,009	48.	7,456
49.	12,345	50.	24,606	51.	34,330	52.	44,004
53.	550,676	54.	677,890	55.	568,900	56.	880,880
57.	2,356,800	58.	5,009,787	59.	8,990,888	60.	7,900,789
61.	22,789,556	62.	66,789,000	63.	33,000,000	64.	56,001,004
65.	345,000,445	66.	667,990,809	67.	112,700,880	68.	230,889,000
69.	1,434,678,990,000	70.	1,000,890,000	71.	2,567,990,008	72.	7,009,667,888

练习2. Listen to and identify the number you hear.

1	B
2	A
3	B
4	C
5	B
6	B
7	A
8	C
9	A
10	C

练习 3. Listen to the dialogue and fill the blanks with a number.

1. 14　2. 700　3. 6,000　4. 19,000,000　5. 7,436,560,000

电话号码（Telephone numbers）

练习 4. Listen and write down the telephone numbers you hear.

1. 94635550　2. 8657765　3. 8657768　4. 7901000
5. 765392　6. 7723281　7. 271963　8. 889740
9. 634096　10. 0999256432　11. 066956462　12. 793225
13. 63343887　14. 016 7455 3242　15. 077691584　16. 99281444
17. 4567890　18. 7896545　19. 2334567　20. 7768876

练习 5. Listen to the dialogue and fill the blanks with a telephone number.

1. 7889089　2. 3445677　3. 2556678　4. 9884577　5. 6779089

邮编与产品编码（Postcode and product model）

练习 6. Listen and write down the postcode you hear.

1.	PL239PU	2.	S154DY	3.	JW142
4.	RH12PE	5.	7338	6.	JO6337
7.	London E11	8.	AC937	9.	YQ181
10.	TQ125CZ	11.	HB23	12.	GW432HA
13.	CO290U	14.	OX351VH	15.	B659
16.	VIT613UL	17.	AL2980	18.	Q493Z
19.	WS62YH	20.	TF274Q5	21.	TY12605
22.	R242	23.	BG241DJ	24.	TO34YU
25.	RA67BU	26.	201A	27.	A21-24
28.	AL142BF	29.	UK765024EG	30.	45PL90

练习 7. Listen to the dialogue and write down the number you hear.

1. PL897NM　2. 789JK90　3. NY2202
4. LD880　5. T400897SQA89

时间（Time）

练习 8. Listen and write down the time you hear.

1. 11:00　2. 11:10　3. 11:15　4. 11:25
5. 11:30　6. 11:45　7. 11:50　8. 12:00
9. 5 sharp　10. 6 o'clock　11. 2:02　12. 1:58
13. 8:09　14. 3:23　15. 23:35　16. 21:45
17. 10:20　18. 9:15 am　19. 3:20 pm　20. Almost 2 o'clock

练习 9. Listen to the dialogue and write down the time you hear.

1. 5:00　2. 1:58-2:02　3. 6:45　4. 10:34 am　5. 7:15

年月日、星期（Year-Month-Date）

练习 10. Listen to the following expressions and write them down.

1.	1957	2.	1960
3.	1983	4.	2008
5.	2010	6.	506
7.	32 BC	8.	1980s
9.	1400s	10.	1860s
11.	22nd October	12.	14th September
13.	23rd June	14.	17th October
15.	28th June	16.	February 17th
17.	May 25th	18.	November 1st
19.	13th January, 1974	20.	27th March, 1972

练习 11. Listen to the dialogue and fill the blanks.

1. November 2nd, 2010
2. December 9, 2010
3. May the thirteenth
4. June 14th, next year
5. Friday

钱币（Money）

练习 12. Listen and write down what you hear.

1. 4.45 pounds
2. 29.5 dollars
3. 319 pounds
4. 450 dollars
5. 25 pence
6. 50 dollars
7. 4.60 pounds
8. 6.20 pounds
9. 5.99 pounds
10. 26.75 pounds

练习 13. Listen to the dialogue and finish the tasks.

1. 123 pounds
2. 7,500 pounds
3. about 25 pounds
4. $23.50
5. about 3 pounds
6. $34.50
7. 21.60 pounds.
8. 10,000 pounds
9. 300 pounds
10. 15 pounds

第一周　星期四　单词拼写

地　名

练习 1. Listen and write down the addresses.

1. 74 North Road
2. 17 Upland Road
3. No. 16 Bridge Road
4. 27 Bank Road
5. West Street
6. 42 South Street
7. 21A Eagle Road
8. 15 Station Avenue
9. 32 Bank Street
10. 8 Hill Road
11. West Avenue
12. 40 Long Road
13. Bank House
14. No.2 Gold Street
15. 48 North Avenue
16. London Lane
17. 84 Park Road
18. 64 Queen Avenue
19. 11 Bridge street
20. 6 Beach Road
21. 124 Green Street
22. 14 Mountain Road

23. 24 River Lane
24. 7 Market Street
25. 84 Park Road
26. 59 Franklyn
27. Hillsdonne Road
28. 6 Doven Road
29. Ellendale
30. Flat 2, Red House, Church Road, Birmingham

练习 2. **Listen to the dialogue and fill in the blanks.**

1. 21 Bristol Square 2. London Lane 3. 24 Hillsdonne Road
4. 46 Kingston Avenue 5. Melbourne Street

人 名

练习 3. **Listen and write down the names your hear.**

1. Helen 2. Kevin 3. John Lee 4. Peter Smith
5. Manuja 6. Yuichini 7. Thorn 8. Urwin
9. Susan Braddle 10. Peter Wisborough 11. Rogala 12. Herdie
13. Milmilinen 14. Akitson 15. Johna Smith

练习 4. **Listen to the dialogue and fill in the blanks.**

1. Paul Smithers 2. Murray Atkins 3. John Whitton
4. Mionst Paynter 5. Jerry Northwaite

第一周 星期五 听写

单 词 听 写

练习 1. **Listen and write down the words you hear.**

1.	forever	2.	honest	3.	christmas
4.	tomb	5.	interviewee	6.	extra
7.	advertisement	8.	scholarship	9.	chemist's
10.	psychology	11.	café	12.	secretary
13.	dormitory	14.	cheque	15.	allergic
16.	accommodation	17.	criminal	18.	register
19.	reference	20.	classical	21.	statistics
22.	librarian	23.	classification	24.	principal
25.	experiment	26.	outstanding	27.	immune
28.	attachment	29.	finance	30.	background

词 组 听 写

练习 2. **Listen and write down the expressions you hear.**

1. I don't know.
2. I can't see.
3. I'll do that.
4. Let me see.
5. Half an hour.
6. I almost forgot.
7. As soon as possible.
8. That sounds great.
9. Let's make it 2 o'clock.
10. Can I help you?

句子听写

练习 3. Listen and write down the sentences you hear, you will listen to the sentences twice.

1. Excuse me, I am conducting a survey about what TV programs people watch. Would you mind answering me a few details?
2. I just need to take down some details.
3. I am calling to see if the house you advertised is still available.
4. I was born in Japan, although I have lived in Singapore for about ten years, but right now I live in America.
5. Have you decided what to do your research project on yet?
6. Good morning, ladies and gentlemen. I am speaking today on behalf of my research team, which consists of two other primary teachers and a doctorial student in addition to myself.
7. Have you finished that presentation we have to give in the seminar on Friday?
8. I am due to begin a course in September and would like to know what type of accommodation you have available.
9. Good morning, listeners. I would like to welcome George Smith, who is going to talk to us about buying a car.
10. In today's session George is going to tell us about his research topic.

段落听写

练习 4. Listen to a short passage introducing the city of Oxford, write down every word you hear. You can listen to the recording for three times.

Oxford is a lively and beautiful city with much to offer both students and visitors. It is about 57 miles northwest of London and has excellent road and rail links to the rest of the UK and all major airports. The total population of Oxford is about 140,000 including over 30,000 students in total from the University of Oxford and the city's other university, Oxford Brookes. As a result, you will find a wealth of cultural, recreational and sports facilities with a busy and cosmopolitan atmosphere. Enchanting historic buildings sit alongside all the main high street stores, numerous coffee shops and restaurants, and a thriving bar and club scene. Oxford also boasts a surprising amount of green spaces, including beautiful waterways that you can walk alongside or punt down, the oldest botanic garden in the country, the University parks, and individual college gardens.

练习 5. Listen to the recording and fill in the blanks according to what you hear.

1. the form of a letter
2. candidate's academic fitness
3. suitability
4. be relevant to
5. the candidate's recent study
6. the standard
7. application deadline
8. confidential
9. Data Protection Act
10. copy

练习 6. Listen to the recording and complete the summary of the article you hear.

1. 40
2. faculties
3. departments
4. institutions

5. second
6. 120
7. 2,490
8. older
9. one-stop search
10. type, format or location
11. online catalogue
12. subject areas
13. electronic text archives
14. image databases
15. departmental and museum

第一周 星期六 听对话

练习 1. Listen to the dialogue and finish the tasks.

Dialogue 1	B	Dialogue 2	C	Dialogue 3	A
Dialogue 4	CB	Dialogue 5	AB	Dialogue 6	C
Dialogue 7	BC	Dialogue 8	AB	Dialogue 9	can't afford to
Dialogue 10	CC	Dialogue 11	C	Dialogue 12	B
Dialogue 13	C	Dialogue 14	B	Dialogue 15	C/CD
Dialogue 16	C	Dialogue 17	B	Dialogue 18	A
Dialogue 19	B	Dialogue 20 1. By the window; 2. one chicken and chips with baked beans; 3. mint tea; 4. cheese sandwich; 5. coffee			

第一周 星期日 听新闻

练习 1	1. B 2. A
练习 2	1. C 2. A
练习 3	1. D 2. C
练习 4	1. D 2. B 3. A
练习 5	1. A 2. B
练习 6	1. emergency budget 2. crime; drug use; unemployment 3. demolished; rebuilt
练习 7	1. deployment 2. pay tribute 3. contributor
练习 8	1. parliament 2. $270 billion 3. immigration
练习 9	1. multi-billion 2. aggravate
练习 10	1. summit 2. financial; technological 3. renewable; nuclear

第二周 题型渗透听力策略

第二周 星期一 填表题

Example 1 *Questions 1-7*

1. Urwin
2. 54 Bristol Square
3. RH12PE
4. Japanese
5. Weekends
6. Action movies
7. Comedies

Example 2 *Questions 1-9*

1. John Whitton
2. 17 Market Street
3. 3849950

4. May 14th, 1979 5. IT 6. 24,000
7. Married 8. Nurse 9. Buy a car

Example 3 *Questions 1-10*

1. Grieg 2. 15th of the third month 1980
3. M528T 4. Singapore
5. One year 6. One
7. Back door 8. computer & purse
9. QS41885377020 10. Silver

第二周 星期二 多选题

Example 1 *Questions 1-4*

1. B 2. B 3. AC 4. C

Example 2 *Questions 1-5*

1. B 2. C 3. A 4. B 5. B

Example 3 *Questions 1-7*

1. A 2. C 3. B 4. B 5. A 6. B 7. C

第二周 星期三 填图题

Example 1

1. Information desk 2. Reference room 3. Seminar room
4. Newspaper area 5. DVD area

Example 2

1. Administration building (F) 2. Conference building (B) 3. Teaching building (J)
4. Café (E) 5. Canteen (C) 6. Garden (D)
7. Dormitory (I) 8. Playground (H) 9. Library (A)
10. Side gate (G)

第二周 星期四 完成句子

Example 1 *Questions 1-10*

1. 3 years old 2. Other children 3. 3 months/ 5 years 4. Cooperative
5. Training 6. Visit 7. Confident 8. $1,200
9. $450 10. Monday/ Friday

Example 2 *Questions 1-8*

1. George Tilts 2. 21st of June 3. Two double rooms 4. Vegetarian
5. Prior arrangement 6. One 7. 26th of June 8. 5:30

Example 3 ***Questions 1-10***

1. 15 to 20
2. 25
3. vegetarians
4. peanuts
5. J
6. £45 per person
7. starters
8. half a bottle
9. Hans Delly
10. 05725 693563

第二周　星期五　补全题

Example 1

1. compulsory
2. four to seven
3. twelve
4. schools
5. basic literacy
6. numeracy
7. science, geography, history

Example 2

1. estate agents
2. builders
3. lenders
4. mortgage lender
5. three times
6. Building Society
7. banks
8. Internet
9. telephone lenders
10. overheads

Example 3

1. steam engines
2. wheels
3. 1804
4. five miles
5. WWII
6. privatized
7. infrastructure
8. government
9. two out of ten
10. complaints

第二周　星期六　配对题

Example 1 ***Questions 1-4***

1-4：DBCA

Example 2 ***Questions 6-10***

6-10：CACBC

第二周　星期日　简答题

Example 1 ***Questions 1-7***

1. Computer
2. T450
3. Last month
4. Sutton Road store
5. $400
6. It stopped working
7. Last Tuesday

Example 2 ***Questions 1-10***

1. Go to concert
2. Have a dinner
3. City center
4. Japanese food/ sashimi
5. It's too expensive
6. Eastern café
7. 9:40
8. At bus stop
9. 3655 9889
10. 412

Example 3 ***Questions 1-5***

1. Travelling
2. Phased retirement
3. Flexible
4. E-learning
5. Yes

第三周 常考场景精练

第三周 星期一 租房

场景一：电话找房

1. tenth 2. subway station 3. cat 4. C 5. B
6. A 7. B 8. C 9. Melbourne 10. 34 Bath Road

场景二：向朋友咨询租房

1. B 2. C 3. C 4. the East Side 5. $400 6. C

场景三：与房东谈论租房

1. Changed 2. Two days 3. C 4. C
5. A 6. A 7. B 8. C

第三周 星期二 学校

场景一：语言学习

1. connected to 2. more effective 3. words and phrases
4. take responsibility 5. guarantee

场景二：课程咨询

1. B 2. D 3. C 4. 9694 5. Monday afternoons 6. C

场景三：图书馆预约书

1. Thomas Green 2. Expired membership 3. 21 Southern Avenue
4. 66674694 5. A 6. B

第三周 星期三 旅行

场景一：与朋友谈论度假计划

1. Needs a break 2. B 3. C 4. B
5. A 6. Brand View 7. B 8. AD

场景二：导游介绍伦敦塔轶事

1. William the Conqueror/ the King 2. execution
3. would-be traitors 4. A
5. Westminster Abbey 6. B

场景三：旅游公司合作

1. 9 AM 2. 12 3. A 4. C 5. B

第三周 星期四 健康和医疗

场景一：牙齿健康调查

1. C 2. A 3. C 4. B 5. an hour 6. C 7. C

场景二：节食

1. lose weight 2. a nutrition balance 3. little nutritional value 4. carbohydrates
5. C 6. C 7. C 8. B

场景三：中西医

1. Acupuncture/ holistic medicine 2. overall health
3. symptoms 4. root cause
5. A 6. C

第三周 星期五 生活

场景一：讨论生日聚会

1. Wednesday 2. joint birthday party 3. B 4. A
5. C 6. C 7. C

场景二：有机牛排

1. C 2. B 3. A 4. A 5. A

场景三：看朋友的孩子

1. August the tenth 2. Tom Whitehead 3. four and a quarter kilos 4. curly black hair
5. 25 Bluefield Road 6. C 7. B

第三周 星期六 环保

场景一：回收电池

1. eight batteries 2. nickel 3. Automotive
4. Rechargeable 5. motorcycles

场景二：保护宠物免受野生动物攻击

1. B 2. 5.5 3. outdoors 4. scare away
5. food or garbage 6. domestic dogs

场景三：温室效应

1. greenhouse gasses 2. bands of wavelengths
3. less and less 4. overlap
5. water vapor 6. the largest
7. concentration

第三周　星期日　科研

场景一：讨论科研

1. print　2. by themselves　3. radios　4. audio-visual
5. all the students　6. electronic

场景二：论文写作

1. orient　2. goodwill
3. alert　4. scope
5. interpreting and approaching　6. context
7. focus　8. conclusion
9. culturally diverse workplace　10. multiculturalism
11. diverse cultures　12. non-verbal communication

场景三：申请项目基金

1. C　2. A　3. A　4. Dad and mum/ parents
5. B　6. C　7. B

第四周　七天模拟，强力冲刺

第四周　星期一　Model Test 1

SECTION 1 *Questions 1-10*

1. Acacia Avenue　2. RA67BU　3. photography　4. they moved
5. nursery　6. restaurant/ waitress　7. A　8. B
9. A　10. C

SECTION 2 *Questions 11-20*

11. only recently　12. flexible　13. practical skills/ theoretical knowledge
14. national　15. B　16. C　17. B
18. nearly 200　19. 25%　20. 15%

SECTION 3 *Questions 21-30*

21. language learning strategies　22. pleased/ happy/ satisfied
23. the internet　24. B
25. C　26. C
27. computer/ making diagrams　28. transitional
29. length　30. before next Friday

SECTION 4 *Questions 31-40*

31. A　32. B　33. 1863　34. automobiles
35. gearing　36. dropped　37. balloon　38. narrower
39. three-speed　40. accessories

第四周　星期二　Model Test 2

SECTION 1 *Questions 1-10*

1. academic
2. Sundays
3. Two passport-size photos
4. No
5. Two weeks
6. 1,500
7. Exceptional circumstances
8. 13 Supreme Court
9. SW186
10. 2827- 6362

SECTION 2 *Questions 11-20*

11. psychiatric
12. 64 million
13. another disorder
14. a month
15. muscular
16. C
17. A
18. sleeping pills
19. longevity
20. sleep hygiene

SECTION 3 *Questions 21-30*

21. C
22. B
23. A
24. C
25. B
26. treason
27. scientific discovery /religious revival
28. the Victorian era
29. new University Museum
30. 1878

SECTION 4 *Questions 31-40*

31. B
32. 30-90 million years/ millions of years
33. protect the tree
34. low/special gravity
35. oxygen
36. C
37. honey
38. tourism
39. B
40. transparent

第四周　星期三　Model Test 3

SECTION 1 *Questions 1-10*

1. Chinese
2. Kent
3. No
4. Trees and fields
5. C
6. A
7. CD
8. C
9. C
10. C

SECTION 2 *Questions 11-20*

11. A
12. B
13. D
14. A
15. A
16. lock up
17. mid-evening
18. well-lit area
19. driver's license / registration
20. vital statistics

SECTION 3 *Questions 21-30*

21. communicating information
22. borders

23．ministry of communications
24．A
25．B
26．98 percent
27．2 hours
28．A
29．C
30．B

SECTION 4 ***Questions 31-40***

31．unclear
32．River Thames
33．green fields
34．1520
35．taller
36．B
37．A
38．C
39．A
40．C

第四周　星期四　Model Test 4

SECTION 1 ***Questions 1-10***

1．George Tomas
2．October 5th, 1978
3．30 Kinston Street
4．W-H-78093
5．2:00 O'clock/the 16th of July
6．A、
7．C
8．B
9．twenty-four hours
10．city center

SECTION 2 ***Questions 11-20***

11．type of holiday
12．mountain biking
13．accommodation
14．a spa
15．a swimming pool
16．beach huts
17．friends or family members
18．brochures
19．look online
20．hotels

SECTION 3 ***Questions 21-30***

21．B
22．A
23．A
24．library research
25．customers behaviour
26．the internet
27．the second five years
28．C
29．B
30．C

SECTION 4 ***Questions 31-40***

31．unsolved
32．make progress
33．their own sake
34．C
35．B
36．illustration
37．link
38．theoretical
39．optimal
40．superiority

第四周　星期五　Model Test 5

SECTION 1 ***Questions 1-10***

1．Joy Armstrong
2．Ask for quotations
3．Japan
4．32 Westmill Street
5．WS89SC
6．B

7. B
8. C
9. £500
10. £3000

SECTION 2 ***Questions 11-20***

11. Aerobics
12. B
13. F
14. overall physical condition
15. a slower pace
16. food groups
17. Hydration
18. 12 cups
19. adjustment
20. flexibility

SECTION 3 ***Questions 21-30***

21. puzzled
22. self-assess techniques
23. write learning diary
24. negative
25. awful reading
26. A
27. B
28. C
29. helpful/useful
30. patient

SECTION 4 ***Questions 31-40***

31. Population
32. 3,5 billion
33. Expansion
34. entertainment
35. urbanization
36. high-density
37. Climate
38. evaporation
39. pollution
40. raw sewage

第四周　星期六　Model Test 6

SECTION 1 ***Questions 1-10***

1. George Smith
2. 6 Devon Road, Oxford.
3. 634096-54
4. B
5. C
6. C
7. A
8. road map
9. flash light
10. a camp tent

SECTION 2 ***Questions 11-20***

11. retail therapy
12. personal reward
13. your circumstances
14. what to do
15. escape from reality
16. A
17. C
18. doing exercise
19. compliment our choice
20. the reasons

SECTION 3 ***Questions 21-30***

21. radiates energy
22. greenhouse gases
23. A
24. E

25. D
26. ice clouds
27. initial analyses
28. be frozen
29. solar energy
30. Collapse of glaciers

SECTION 4 ***Questions 31-40***

31. A
32. multinational corporations
33. 3500 BC
34. poisonous mercury/lead
35. Church leaders
36. pale-skinned
37. actors
38. delicate flowers
39. $19 billion
40. 1909

第四周 星期日 Model Test 7

SECTION 1 ***Questions 1-10***

1. visa or entry clearance
2. British Missions overseas
3. Home Office
4. C
5. B
6. A
7. A
8. C
9. five minutes
10. 15 working days

SECTION 2 ***Questions 11-20***

11. C
12. B
13. B
14. C
15. A
16. tax relief
17. tax-efficient
18. contributions
19. 25%
20. investments

SECTION 3 ***Questions 21-30***

21. B
22. A
23. B
24. a future term
25. lose the information/ start again
26. 2
27. review
28. at that time
29. "Diploma Address" field
30. confirming

SECTION 4 ***Questions 31-40***

31. C
32. C
33. Wednesday 26 August
34. 6:30pm
35. cross-disciplinary and cross-campus
36. D
37. problem-based approach
38. environmental management
39. enquiry
40. video-conferenced and filmed

附录2 听力原文

第一周 雅思听力基本功训练

第一周 星期三 练习听数字

基数词、序数词、分数、百分数、小数

（cardinal numbers, ordinal numbers, fractions, percentages, decimals）

练习1. Listen to some number and write them down in the table.

1.	15	2.	50	3.	55	4.	67
5.	48	6.	81	7.	80	8.	18
9.	19	10.	28	11.	35	12.	77
13.	90	14.	33	15.	64	16.	89
17.	105	18.	118	19.	115	20.	150
21.	222	22.	345	23.	565	24.	901
25.	999	26.	109	27.	119	28.	190
29.	808	30.	771	31.	442	32.	677
33.	9,000	34.	5,555	35.	1,002	36.	4,667
37.	8,030	38.	4,090	39.	1,234	40.	5,890
41.	7,112	42.	3,337	43.	2,334	44.	6,008
45.	6,006	46.	2,111	47.	3,009	48.	7,456
49.	12,345	50.	24,606	51.	34,330	52.	44,004
53.	550,676	54.	677,890	55.	568,900	56.	880,880
57.	2,356,800	58.	5,009,787	59.	8,990,888	60.	7,900,789
61.	22,789,556	62.	66,789,000	63.	33,000,000	64.	56,001,004
65.	345,000,445	66.	667,990,809	67.	112,700,880	68.	230,889,000
69.	1,434,678,990,000	70.	1,000,890,000	71.	2,567,990,008	72.	7,009,667,888

练习2. Listen to and identify the number you hear.

1	50
2	180
3	318
4	4,566
5	70,890
6	713,566
7	7,344,600
8	14,500,617
9	590,590,950
10	9,333,440,600

练习 3．Listen to the dialogue and fill the blanks with a number.

1．A: May I know how old you are?
B: I will be 15 next year.

2．A: How many people can this auditorium hold?
B: I think maybe 700.

3．A: How much do you have to pay every year?
B: Well, it's about $5,500, but I will have to pay another $500 for course books.

4．A: Do you happen to know the population of this city?
B: Yes, it's about 19,000,000.

5．A: How many books are there in that reading room?
B: Well, let me see, yes, It is here, it's 7,436,560,000 in total.

电话号码（**Telephone numbers**）

练习 4．Listen and write down the telephone numbers you hear.

1．94635550	2．8657765	3．8657768	4．7901000
5．765392	6．7723281	7．271963	8．889740
9．634096	10．0999256432	11．066956462	12．793225
13．63343887	14．016 7455 3242	15．077691584	16．99281444
17．4567890	18．7896545	19．2334567	20．7768876

练习 5．Listen to the dialogue and fill the blanks with a telephone number.

1．A: May I know your phone number please?
B: That's 7889089.

2．A: What is your office number?
B: My office number is 3345677. No, I always make that wrong. It's 3445677.

3．A: How shall I contact you?
B: You can reach us at 2556678.

4．A: Do you know Professor Smith's telephone number?
B: Yes, I think it is in my mobile, yes, it's 9884577.

5．A: 6779089, who is talking?
B: I am sorry, I dialed a wrong number.

邮编与产品编码（**Postcode and product model**）

练习 6．Listen and write down the postcode you hear.

1．PL239PU　　2．S154DY　　3．JW142

4. RH12PE	5. 7338	6. JO6337
7. London E11	8. AC937	9. YQ181
10. TQ125CZ	11. HB23	12. GW432HA
13. CO290U	14. OX351VH	15. B659
16. VIT613UL	17. AL2980	18. Q493Z
19. WS62YH	20. TF274Q5	21. TY12605
22. R242	23. BG241DJ	24. TO34YU
25. RA67BU	26. 201A	27. A21-24
28. AL142BF	29. UK765024EG	30. 45PL90

练习 7. Listen to the dialogue and write down the number you hear.

1. A: And your postcode?
   B: It's PL897NM.

2. A: Your postcode is 789JK90, is that right?
   B: Yes, correct.

3. A: Good morning, I am calling to tell you that my postcode has been changed now.
   B: OK, what's that?
   A: It's NY2202, please make sure you use the new one.
   B: OK, I will do.

4. A: I am sending a postcard to George, do you know his postcode?
   B: Yes, the letter he wrote to me last week says it's LD880.

5. A: Do you still remember the serial number of your lost computer?
   B: Sure, I can never forget, it's T400897SQA89.

时间（**Time**）

练习 8. Listen and write down the time you hear.

1. 11:00	2. 11:10	3. 11:15	4. 11:25
5. 11:30	6. 11:45	7. 11:50	8. 12:00
9. 5 sharp	10. 6 o'clock	11. 2:02	12. 1:58
13. 8:09	14. 3:23	15. 23:35	16. 21:45
17. 10:20	18. 9:15 a.m.	19. 3:20 p.m.	20. almost 2 o'clock

练习 9. Listen to the dialogue and write down the time you hear.

1. A: Excuse me, do you have time?
   B: Yes, it's almost 5 o'clock.

2. A: At what time will the train stop in this station?
   B: Well it's about two to two to two two.

3. A:When shall we meet tomorrow?

B: How about 6:45?

A: That's fine with me.

4. A: Excuse me, when will the plane arrive at London?

B: Well, it's about 10:34 am.

5. A: Good evening, what can I do for you?

B: Yes, I want to book an alarm call next morning at 7:15.

A: No problem, I will call you on time, good night.

B: Thank you.

年月日、星期（Year-Month-Date）

练习 10. Listen to the following expressions and write them down.

1. 1957	2. 1960	3. 1983	4. 2008
5. 2010	6. 506	7. 32 BC	8. 1980s
9. 1400s	10. 1860s	11. 22nd October	12. 14th September
13. 23rd June	14. 17th October	15. 28th June	16. February 17th
17. May 25th	18. November 1st	19. 13th January, 1974	20. 27th March, 1972

练习 11. Listen to the dialogue and fill in the blanks.

1. A: Excuse me, what's the date today?

B: It's November 2nd, 2010.

2. A: When would you leave Australia?

B: Well, my flight is on December 9, 2010.

3. A: What day is today?

B: Today is Tuesday, May the thirteenth.

4. A: What's the deadline of our thesis?

B: It's June 14th, next year.

5. A: Are you free this Friday? Would you come to my house and have a dinner with us?

B: Thank you so much. I really want to, but I have to see my brother off, he is going back to China that day.

钱币（Money）

练习 12. Listen and write down what you hear.

1. 4.45 pounds	2. 29.50 dollars	3. 319 pounds	4. 450 dollars
5. 25 pence	6. 50 dollars	7. 4.60 pounds	8. 6.20 pounds
9. 5.99 pounds	10. 26.75 pounds		

练习 13. Listen to the dialogue and finish the tasks.

1. A: How much is the rent each month, please?
   B: It's 30 pounds per week, and you have to pay 3 pounds for laundry, so that's 123 pounds in total.

2. A: How much is the tuition fee?
   B: That depends on what course you take, it's generally cost about 6,000 to 8,000 pounds.
   A: What is the tuition for Geography courses every year?
   B: That's about 7,000 pounds, plus 500 pounds for textbooks.

3. A: I am new here. Do you know how much I should tip the waiter?
   B: It's generally 10 percent of your expenses.
   A: I see. It's about 250 pounds tonight, so I should give him 25 pounds, is that right?
   B: Yes, you can give more if you like, of course.

4. Customer: OK, here is the parcel, how much postage shall I pay?
   Post Officer: Well, let me weigh it first … yes, it's $23.50.
   Customer: Thank you.

5. A: Do you know what's the general fare for subway in London?
   B: Well, I am not sure. I often drive, but I guess it's about 3 pounds or so.
   A: Thank you.

6. A: How much did they charge you for that?
   B: They charged me $34.50.
   A: Oh, really, you were overcharged, I think.

7. A: Would you go to the circus next Saturday?
   B: Well, it sounds interesting. What's the admission?
   A: It's 21 pounds sixty.
   B: Wow, that's expensive, I don't think it worths it.

8. A: Why don't you study in UK for a year as well?
   B: Well, I want to, but it is expensive. What is your expense every year?
   A: It's about 10,000 pounds except tuition fee.
   B: Oh, dear. I will have to save more money.

9. A: I want to rent a car for a week, how much is the rent?
   B: It's 50 pounds a day, but you only need to pay for 300 for seven days.

10. A: Excuse me, how much is the fee for me?
    B: Let me see, three bottles of aspirin, that's 15 pounds in total.

第一周　星期四　单词拼写

地　名

练习 1. Listen and write down the addresses.

1. 74 North Road	2. 17 Upland Road	3. No. 16 Bridge Road
4. 27 Bank Road	5. West Street	6. 42 South Street
7. 21A Eagle Road	8. 15 Station Avenue	9. 32 Bank Street
10. 8 Hill Road	11. West Avenue	12. 40 Long Road
13. Bank House	14. No.2 Gold Street	15. 48 North Avenue
16. London Lane	17. 84 Park Road	18. 64 Queen Avenue
19. 11 Bridge street	20. 6 Beach Road	21. 124 Green Street
22. 14 Mountain Road	23. 24 River Lane	24. 7 Market Street
25. 84 Park Road	26. 59 Franklyn	27. Hillsdonne Road
28. 6 Doven Road	29. Ellendale	30. Flat 2, Red House, Church Road, Birmingham

练习 2. Listen to the dialogue and fill in the blanks.

1. A: What's your address please?
   B: 21 Bristol Square.

2. A: Where do you live please?
   B: I live on London Lane.

3. A: Where shall I send your ticket to?
   B: Can you please send it to 24 Hillsdonne Road, that's H-I-L-L-S-D-O-N-N-E.
   A: That's no problem.

4. A: Where are you now? I can pick you up there.
   B: I am, let me see, yes, at 46 Kingston Avenue.
   A: I will be there in 20 minutes.

5. A: Excuse me, is the apartment you advertised still available?
   B: Yes.
   A: Can I have a look at it please?
   B: Sure.
   A: Can you tell me where it is please?
   B: It's on Melbourne Street.
   A: Thank you.

人　名

练习 3. Listen and write down the names your hear.

1. Helen　　2. Kevin

3. John Lee
4. Peter Smith
5. Manuja: M-A-N-U-J-A
6. Yuichini: Y-U-I-C-H-I-N-I
7. Thorn: T-H-O-R-N
8. Urwin: U-R-W-I-N
9. Susan Braddle: B-R-A-D-D-L-E
10. Peter Wisborough: W-I-S-B-O-R-O-U-G-H
11. Rogala:R-O-G-A-L-A
12. Herdie: H-E-R-D-I-E
13. Milmilinen: M-I-L-M-I-L-I-N-E-N
14. Akitson: A-K-I-T-S-O-N
15. Johna Smith: J-O-H-N-A

练习 4. Listen to the dialogue and fill in the blanks.

1. A: I just need to take down some details. What's your name please?
   B: My name is Paul Smithers.
   A: How do you spell that?
   B: Paul is P-A-U-L, Smithers is S-M-I-T-H-E-R-S.

2. A: Good morning, I would like to apply for a new library card, please?
   B: Sure, may I know you name please?
   A: Murray Atkins.
   B: How do you spell your name please?
   A: Murray, M-U-R-R-A-Y, Atkins is A-T-K-I-N-S.
   B: Thank you, and your …

3. A: Good morning, I would like to apply for a loan please.
   B: OK, I just need to take down some details. Can you tell me your name please?
   A: Sure, my name is John Whitton. W-H-I-T-T-O-N, Whitton.
   B: And your address…

4. A: …OK, that's pretty much the information about the house, you can always come to take a look.
   B: Thank you very much. May I come tomorrow?
   A: Sure, I am always at home. What's your name again?
   B: Mionst Paynter, that's M-I-O-N-S-T, MIONST, P-A-Y-N-T-E-R, Paynter.
   A: Good, you can come at 9 o'clock or so.
   B: Thank you.

5. A: Good morning, I am calling to see if the job vacancy you advertised is still available?
   B: Yes, we had several applicants, but I think we can still give you the chance for interview if you like.
   A: That will be great.
   B: What's your name please?
   A: My name is Jerry Northwaite, my last name is N-O-R-T-H-W-A-I-T-E.
   B: Thank you. Can you come at ten o'clock tomorrow morning…

星期五 听写

单词听写

练习 1. Listen and write down the words you hear.

1. forever	2. honest	3. christmas
4. tomb	5. interviewee	6. extra
7. advertisement	8. scholarship	9. chemist's
10. psychology	11. café	12. secretary
13. dormitory	14. cheque	15. allergic
16. accommodation	17. criminal	18. register
19. reference	20. classical	21. statistics
22. librarian	23. classification	24. principal
25. experiment	26. annul	27. immune
28. attachment	29. outstanding	30. background

词组听写

练习 2. Listen and write down the expressions you hear.

1. I don't know.	2. I can't see.
3. I'll do that.	4. Let me see.
5. Half an hour.	6. I almost forgot.
7. As soon as possible.	8. That sounds great.
9. Let's make it 2 o'clock.	10. Can I help you?

句子听写

练习 3. Listen and write down the sentences you hear, you will listen to the sentences twice.

1. Excuse me, but I am conducting a survey about what TV programs people watch. Would you mind answering me a few details?
2. I just need to take down some details.
3. I am calling to see if the house you advertised is still available.
4. I was born in Japan, although I have lived in Singapore for about ten years, but right now I live in America.
5. Have you decided what to do your research project on yet?
6. Good morning, ladies and gentlemen. I am speaking today on behalf of my research team, which consists of two other primary teachers and a doctorial student in addition to myself.
7. Have you finished that presentation we have to give in the seminar on Friday?
8. I am due to begin a course in September and would like to know what type of accommodation you have available.
9. Good morning, listeners. I would like to welcome George Smith, who is going to talk to us about buying a car.

10. In today's session George is going to tell us about his research topic.

段 落 听 写

练习 4. Listen to a short passage introducing the city of Oxford, write down every word you hear. You can listen to the recording for three times.

Oxford is a lively and beautiful city with much to offer both students and visitors. It is about 57 miles northwest of London and has excellent road and rail links to the rest of the UK and all major airports. The total population of Oxford is about 140,000 including over 30,000 students in total from the University of Oxford and the city's other university, Oxford Brookes. As a result, you will find a wealth of cultural, recreational and sports facilities with a busy and cosmopolitan atmosphere. Enchanting historic buildings sit alongside all the main high street stores, numerous coffee shops and restaurants, and a thriving bar and club scene. Oxford also boasts a surprising amount of green spaces, including beautiful waterways that you can walk alongside or punt down, the oldest botanic garden in the country, the University parks, and individual college gardens.

练习 5. Listen to the recording and fill in the blanks according to what you hear.

INFORMATION FOR REFEREES

References should be supplied in the form of a letter. Referees should comment on the candidate's academic fitness and general suitability for the proposed programme of study.

Referees should also supply any other information they consider to be relevant to the candidate's application and where they have knowledge of the candidate's recent study it would be helpful if they could indicate the standard achieved.

All references must be received by the relevant application deadline.

The reference supplied will be treated as confidential, subject to the provisions of the UK Data Protection Act of 1998. If the candidate requests to see the reference, we may need to provide a copy.

练习 6. listen to the recording and complete the summary of the article you hear.

Oxford meets the needs of its students, academics and the international research community with a wide range of library services provided by more than 100 libraries, making it the largest university library system in the UK.

Bodleian Libraries is the integrated library service of the University of Oxford. Established in 2000, it comprises nearly 40 libraries. There are major research libraries as well as libraries attached to faculties, departments and other institutions of the University. The combined collections of Bodleian Libraries number more than 11 million printed items, in addition to vast quantities of materials in many other formats.

The Bodleian Library is the University's main research library and is the second largest in the UK after the British Library. It has 120 miles of occupied shelving, 29 reading rooms and 2,490 places for readers.

College Libraries. Every College has its own library, often consisting of a modern, working library and older collections. Further information can be found on individual college websites.

Search Oxford Libraries Online, SOLO in short, is now the main search engine for library collections. It offers a one-stop search and delivery solution for quickly accessing Oxford's main library information resources regardless of type, format, or location. Search results are presented with a wide array of additional links to improve resource discovery.

Oxford Libraries Information System. All Oxford libraries participate in the online catalogue. It contains records for nearly seven million of the estimated ten million titles held by libraries associated with Oxford University.

E-resources. University libraries share an extensive range of e-resources across all subject areas.

Oxford Digital Library. Oxford is actively involved in developing electronic information, including electronic text archives and image databases. Through the Oxford Digital Library, the University is a leader in the digitisation of manuscripts and other library material.

Oxford University Libraries A-Z. The University also houses many departmental and museum libraries, such as the Museum of the History of Science Library and Oxford University Museum of Natural History Library — Hope Library. Further information about these, and all other University libraries, can be found using the "Libraries A-Z" index.

第一周 星期六 听对话

练习 1. Listen to the dialogue and finish the tasks.

Dialogue 1

Cathy: Let's take a coffee break, shall we?

Watalabe: I wish I could, but I can't.

Cathy: What keeps you so busy? You've been sitting there for hours. You can't just stay on computer forever.

Watalabe: Well, I'm up to my neck in work. I've got to finish this report. Fiona needs it by noon.

Cathy: I understand that, but you'd feel better if you took a break, even for just a short while.

Dialogue 2

Fiona: This was a very good meeting.

Tom: I'm happy that we've finally cleared up some problems.

Fiona: I think we have. Is there anything else to discuss?

Tom: No, that's all, I guess.

Fiona: Then, let's call it a day, shall we?

Tom: I have been waiting for you to say that.

Dialogue 3

Sahara: Hi, Truman, do you think it's possible for us to have a talk sometime about our group presentation today?

Truman: I'd love to, but I've got a pretty tight schedule today.

Sahara: Oh, what have you got going on?

Truman: Well, I've got to finish my research proposal by ten. Then I have to drive to the railway station to pick up a friend of mine at 10:30. After that, I'll have lunch with him. I don't think I can finish that until two o'clock. But then from three until five, I have to go to talk to Professor Wang about my proposal.

Sahara: OK, maybe sometime tomorrow.

Dialogue 4

Roy: Has Brain shown up yet?

Douglas: Nope. I guess something might have come up.

Roy: I wonder what happened.

Douglas: I don't know. I hope it's nothing serious.

Roy: Last week his sister was admitted to the hospital.

Douglas: Oh? What happened?

Roy: His sister had a car accident last week.

Douglas: Is she fine now?

Roy: She's still in a coma.

Douglas: Oh, poor brain. His sister is the only he has left since his parents died last year.

Dialogue 5

Jill: Roger, can you give me a hand right now?

Roger: I'm sorry I can't. I'm tied up with something now.

Jill: Oh, are you on the stupid net again? When are you going to get off?

Roger: Just a second, Dear! I'm looking at a gift site. I wanna make sure I get the right gift for your birthday, don't I?

Jill: Oh? I'm sorry to bother you. Take as much time as you need.

Roger: No problem.

Dialogue 6

A: Where are you heading in such a rush?

B: I'm heading home.

A: Are we still going to have group study tonight?

B: Yeah. I'm just going to grab something to eat and then I'll come back to school.

A: See you then.

B: OK.

Dialogue 7

Laura: What happened just now, Bush? You weren't very kind when you were talking with Mark. What do you have against him?

Bush: I just don't like him.

Laura: Why? What happened?

Bush: Well, you know, last week I went to his office to ask him for some help, and he simply turned up his nose at me! I was so angry that I even don't want to mention his name again!

Laura: Come on. Boy. let it go.

Bush: I know you're right, but somehow I just can't bring myself to forget it.

Dialogue 8

A: Oh, what happened to your face? It looks awful.

B: It's a razor burn. I cut myself when I shaved this morning.

A: Oh, dear. Maybe you could shave in the shower. The steam will help to soften your beard and moustache.

B: Hm, sounds like a good idea.

A: And you should avoid pressing too hard while shaving.

B: I guess I've been stretching it too often when I shave.

A: Hm. I would also suggest you try this cream next time when you shave.

Dialogue 9

A: What are the chances of getting a raise this year?

B: Chances are slim!

A: Wow! You haven't gotten a raise for years?

B: Yeah, three years! The company can't afford to give anyone a raise now.

A: Did you ever think of working somewhere else?

B: Sure. In fact, I have an interview next Friday.

A: Good luck!

Dialogue 10

Woman: Honey, don't you think you should take a vacation? Even one or two days would be fine.

Man: There's no way. There's too much work.

Woman: But you look so exhausted. You need a break!

Man: I know. But we don't have enough people in the company.

Woman: Why don't they hire more people then?

Man: No way. They always try to keep the cost down.

Woman: Maybe you should talk to the manager.

Man: Yes. I'm going to bring this up in tomorrow's meeting.

Dialogue 11

Man: So, how was your interview?

Woman: I haven't gone to the interview yet. It's this afternoon. I'm quite nervous about it.

Man: Don't worry. You have the experience, you will do it well.

Woman: I hope so, but do you have any suggestions for me?

Man: Well, generally, they want someone who works well with people. You've got to show them how easy-going and personable you are!

Woman: Thanks a lot. I will try.

Dialogue 12

Man: Oh, my! It's really hot! I've never seen such scorching weather in my life!

Woman: Tell me about it. It's like the whole world is broiling.

Man: Oh, look at the thermometer! The temperature has hit 98!

Woman: I hope it's not gonna break into three digits!

Man: But it's already awfully close!

Woman: Well, I just hope it'll level off.

Man: I guess we can't do anything until after dark then.

Woman: I guess so.

Dialogue 13

Visiting a friend

Woman: Take a seat please. Would you like a drink?

Man: Oh, yes please! I'd love a gin and tonic.

Woman: What music would you like to listen to? Would you try some Chinese music? I have just bought some Chinese music.

Man: It's great! Where did you get them, I have never seen any Chinese CDs around?

Woman: Erm — It was in the CD shop in the Central Mall. Do you know that place?

Man: Yes. I often go there. Which floor is it?

Woman: Er, I think it's on the left of the second floor, next to the book section?

Man: I see, I will go and buy some next time.

Dialogue 14

Making an appointment

Man: Are you free tomorrow afternoon? I think we should meet sometime to talk about our assignment.

Woman: No, I'm afraid not. I'm meeting Tom then. How about the fourteenth in the morning?

Man: I'm sorry. I'm attending a meeting then.

Woman: What about the next day?

Man: No. I'm busy then too. I will attend a lecture. Are you free on Thursday afternoon?

Woman: Yes, I think I am. Shall we just meet for lunch?

Man: Good idea!

Dialogue 15

Planning the shopping

Husband: I'm going to the shops in a minute. What do we need?

Wife: We're okay for vegetables but we should stock up on meat. Can you go to the butcher's and get some veal and some beef?

Husband: No problem. We also need bread, so I'll go to the baker's. I'll get a cake for Victor's birthday. We'll need balloons for that too.

Wife: Better visit the supermarket then. We'll need some other things for the party. Get some vanilla ice cream, some butter and some vinegar and twelve bottles of beer.

Husband: Okay. The library's beside the baker's. I'd better take back the videos we borrowed last week. They're overdue.

Wife: I'll see you later then.

Husband: Bye! I'll be back before seven.

Dialogue 16

Man: How are you?

Woman: I'm fine, thanks. How about you?

Man: I'm okay. What are you doing these days?

Woman: Busy at work of course — we've got a big project coming up in Japan. I may have to go to Tokyo in a few weeks.

Man: That's great. When are you starting?

Woman: Probably in a week or two. I'll let you know.

Man: Shall we meet sometime before you go?

Woman: Yeah, maybe, if time permits.

Man: OK, let's keep in contact.

Dialogue 17

June: You look awful. What happened?

Mark: Well, you know, This morning I took my car to the garage to have them check the air-conditioner. They only gave it an once-over, refilled it with some Freon, and charged me 300 bucks!

June: No way, that's like robbery.

Mark: Yeah. And they were rude. They said I didn't know anything about cars, which I don't, but they didn't have to be so blunt!

June: Sounds like you got a raw deal! Maybe you should file a complaint with the Consumer Protection Agency.

Dialogue 18

Man: Hi, how is everything going? I heard you're looking for a new job.

Woman: Yeah. I just had an interview yesterday.

Man: Oh. How did it go?

Woman: I think I did well. They said they would make a decision by this Friday.

Man: This Friday? Looks like they want to hire the person as quickly as possible.

Woman: Yeah! I think so, too.

Man: What are your chances of getting that job?

Woman: Well, the director seems to like me.

Man: Well, good luck, then.

Woman: Thanks.

Dialogue 19

Woman: Hello. Liverpool 6735667.

Man: Hello. Is that Douglas?

Woman: Douglas? No. He doesn't live here any more. He's moved last month.

Man: Never! Do you know his new number?

Woman: Yes. I've got it somewhere. Let me see. Where did I put it? Ah — I remember, it's on the memo. Here it is. Do you have a pen to write it down?

Man: Yes, I do. Go on.

Woman: His home number's 7645984, and his office number is 3984059.

Man: Marvelous! Thanks for your help.

Dialogue 20

Ordering a meal

Mervin: Where shall we sit? Look! There are some free seats in that corner.

John: I prefer the seats by the window, it's cooler.

Mervin: OK. What would you like to eat?

John: I'm hungry. I think I'll have chicken and chips with baked beans. Do you want chicken too?

Mervin: I don't feel like eating any meat today. I'll have a cheese sandwich instead.

John: And what about drinks? Shall we have mint tea?

Mervin: I don't think so, look at the price, It's three dollars sixty cents! I'll have a coffee; it's much cheaper, but you can have a mint tea.

Waiter: Good evening.

John: Good evening. We'll have one chicken and chips with baked beans and one cheese sandwich please.

Waiter: OK, would you like something to drink?

Mervin: Yes, A mint tea and a coffee please.

Waiter: OK. One chicken and chips with beans, one cheese sandwich, a mint tea and a coffee, is that all right?

Mervin: Yes, thank you very much, just make it quick, we are both hungry.

Waiter: No problem.

第一周　星期日　听新闻

练习 1. South Sudanese Want Independence From North

It is difficult to find a person on the street in Juba who says they want to remain a part of Sudan. Many were emphatic about the coming divorce, like Abraham, a 26-year-old student.

"And for us, we the citizens of South Sudan, no one is going to vote for unity," Abraham said.

Asked why they want to break with the north, most say they feel discriminated against and marginalized by their Muslim-Arab compatriots.

Some observers worry that the results of the referendum or the possibility that it could be postponed might lead to renewed violence between north and south. But the southerners VOA talked to, said if there is war it will not be initiated from their side.

Southerners say they will choose independence because they have suffered too much as a unified country and are better off on their own. Then they say, development and prosperity will come to their region.

练习 2. Rare Dance Showcases Indigenous Art Festival in Australia

A rare performance by renowned Aboriginal dancers marked the start of one of Australia's most important festivals of indigenous art. The unique dance of the Gurrir Gurrir people depicts events associated with a devastating tropical cyclone in 1974. The catastrophic event helped create one of Australia's most highly regarded indigenous art movements.

The ceremony performed by the Gurrir Gurrir people remembers events surrounding Cyclone Tracy, which devastated Darwin in northern Australia. Aborigines saw the 1974 disaster as a warning from ancient spirits that their culture must not be allowed to wither and die in the face of European colonization.

The spirits were said to have imparted new songs and dances aimed at maintaining the diversity of indigenous culture and the Warmun artistic tradition was born.

Warrmarn-Kija Aborigines perform the Gurrir Gurrir ceremony to open the "Art and Soul" exhibition at the Art Gallery of New South Wales in Sydney, 1 Oct 2010.

练习 3. Workers' Strikes Hit London

Strikes taking place across London have closed down major transport routes and turned transport links into chaos.

London's tube workers went on a 24-hour strike starting Monday evening that left commuters struggling to make it work Tuesday morning.

Thousands of workers on London's transport system walked out because they say proposed job cuts will hurt the service and create safety risks.

British Union leader Crow says workers across Europe are fighting for their rights. "Workers in France are fighting back, they're fighting back all over the place — Greece, in Ireland, in

Portugal, in Spain," added Crow. "And it's quite clear that people are not prepared to be pushed around, they're prepared to stand up and fight."

In London, the strike was set to carry on into the evening. Tuesday afternoon, one worker said she was dreading the commute home.

London's tube workers have more strikes planned for October and November.

练习 4. World Bank Says Population Growth, Climate Change Demand Better Water Management

A soaring world population, climate change and greater demands for food are placing greater demands on the planet's water resources. The World Bank says the best way to address those issues is to have better information and a more integrated approach to water management.

The bank says a review of its 2003 water resources strategy finds many successes in water projects. But it also sets priorities and makes recommendations as access to water becomes critical for many people around the world.

Other recommendations include putting water management higher on the climate change agenda and increase efforts to improve sanitation.

The review also calls for support for hydro power. World Bank Water Sector Manager Julia Bucknall says hydropower could mean building dams but also could mean making better use of existing dams or rehabilitating them.

Inger Andersen, vice-president for sustainable development at the World Bank, says, "Only 23 percent of hydropower potential located in developing countries has been exploited. The gains for the poor can be enormous."

练习 5. BP: Cement Plug Functioning.

The oil company BP says the cement poured into the blown-out Gulf of Mexico oil well is performing well and work has resumed on the relief well designed to kill the ruptured well for good.

BP Chief Operating Officer Doug Suttles says the relief well operation is expected to be completed by mid-August. He said BP's focus is now on clean-up operations that have moved closer to shore, focusing on beaches and wetlands.

BP crews capped the leaking well in mid-July, stopping the leak for the first time since it began in late April. But the cap was meant to be a temporary fix. Officials fear more than 1 million barrels of oil remain in the environment.

Oil began gushing into the Gulf in April when the Deepwater Horizon drill rig exploded, killing 11 workers.

U.S. scientists estimate that nearly 5 million barrels of oil leaked from the damaged well, making it the largest accidental release of oil into water in history, burned or had broken down naturally.

BP faces about $30 billion in cleanup costs.

练习 6. Britain Makes Huge Cuts to Avert Debt Crisis

Britain's new coalition government has passed an emergency budget after warning the state of the country's finances is much worse than expected .

The Clapham Park Estate was once voted one of the worst social housing developments in London. The window frames are crumbling, the apartments are dark and damp and the estate suffers from high levels of crime, drug use and unemployment. Many of the residents are reliant on state handouts to get by. They are places like this that could be hit hardest by cuts in housing and social benefit.

The apartment blocks were due to be demolished and rebuilt, but the money has run out.

Britain's new chancellor, George Osborne of the Conservative Party, claims the previous Labor Party administration took the country to the edge of bankruptcy.

In an emergency budget he outlined, public spending will be cut by one quarter over five years, heralding widespread job losses in the public sector and cuts to Britain's welfare state.

The new budget has been met with angry protests.

练习 7. British Leader Vows Afghan Mission Unchanged

The killing of the British personnel by a lone Afghan policeman at a military compound in Helmand province has raised more questions in Britain about the deployment. It is the latest bad news for the Brown government that already has faced strong criticism here about the war.

Addressing fellow politicians in the House of Commons Wednesday, a somber Prime Minister Gordon Brown paid tribute to the fallen.

"I'm sure the whole House will wish to join me in sending our condolences to the families and friends of the five soldiers who have died in Afghanistan yesterday," he said. " The death of five brave soldiers in a single incident is a terrible and tragic loss and I want to pay tribute, as the whole House will, to their professionalism and to their courage and service," he said.

While he says the deadly incident is being thoroughly investigated, Mr. Brown said the so-called partnering program of training Afghan police and soldiers will go on.

Britain is the second highest contributor to the NATO force in Afghanistan. Some 9,000 are deployed there, training Afghan security personnel and fighting the Taliban.

练习 8. Queen Elizabeth Formally Opens Britain's Parliament

Britain's Queen Elizabeth II has formally opened parliament in a traditional ceremony full of pomp and circumstance. The queen presented the government's program, this year proving especially interesting as Britain's new coalition government outlined its plans to include tough budget cuts.

The queen's speech outlined the government's plans and program, and was put together by the country's officials.

Her words today were written by Britain's new coalition government and emphasized the need for budget cuts.

Britain is estimated to be facing more than $270 billion in debt. On Monday, leaders announced plans to cut more than $7 billion from this year's budget.

Also on the new Conservative-Liberal Democrat legislative agenda was the topic of immigration.

With regard to foreign policy, Queen Elizabeth lent her support to the country's armed forces and called for a defense and security review of military operations.

The British monarch announced more than 20 new bills, which legislators will work to enact during the next 18 months.

练习 9. Australia Blocks China Mine Bid on Security

Australia has vetoed a multi-billion dollar mining project involving a Chinese company because of national security and safety concerns. The plan involved a mining site within a restricted missile testing range at Woomera in the South Australian desert.

The Hawks Nest iron ore mine would have been a joint venture between Australian company Western Plains Resources and a Chinese steel corporation. The plan was to develop a multi-billion dollar iron ore facility inside the Woomera Prohibited Area, a military testing base in South Australia, where other mining projects have been approved in the past.

The application has been blocked by the Australian government, which has cited national security and safety concerns.

This latest decision could aggravate relations between Canberra and Beijing. China has become one of the biggest buyers of Australian exports, particularly commodities such as iron ore. But the failure of a Chinese offer to buy a large stake in Australian mining company Rio Tinto, followed by China's arrest of Rio Tinto executives on industrial espionage charges, caused new tension between the two.

练习 10. A Summit on climate change at the United Nations

Nearly 100 world leaders met at a summit at the United Nations Tuesday to put their political weight behind achieving a global climate treaty later this year when they meet in the Danish capital.

U. N. Secretary-General Ban Ki-moon launched the unprecedented summit with a warning to world leaders that their decisions would have "momentous consequences." "The fate of future generations, and the hopes and livelihoods of billions today, rest, literally, with you," he said.

He urged action this December when the international community meets in Copenhagen. Mr. Ban said a successful deal would be one that includes ambitious reduction targets from industrialized countries and commitments on emissions from developing ones. He said it should also include financial and technological support for emerging countries.

The United States and China are each responsible for about one-fifth of carbon emissions worldwide, so it came as good news when China's President Hu Jintao announced plans to cut emissions significantly by 2020, and to vigorously develop renewable and nuclear energy.

第二周　题型渗透听力策略

第二周　星期一　填表题

Example 1

Questions 1-7

Complete the notes below.

Write ***NO MORE THAN THREE WORDS AND/OR A NUMBER*** *for each answer.*

A: Excuse me, I'm conducting a survey about the types of movies people watch. Would you mind answering a few questions?

B: No, not at all.

A: Can you tell me your name please?

B: It's Urwin. That's U-R-W-I-N.

A: And where do you live?

B: 54 Bristol Square.

A: Bristol Square. OK, and your postcode?

B: RH12PE.

A: And can you tell me where you're from please?

B: Sure, I was born in Tokyo.

A: When do you normally watch movies?

B: Well, I am very busy during the weekdays, so it's generally at the weekend.

A: What kind of movies do you often watch?

B: I like action movies, especially the James Bond movies. Other than that, mainly comedies.

A: Thank you very much for your time.

B: You are welcome.

Example 2

Questions 1-9

A: Good afternoon, sir. How may I help you?

B: I'd like to apply for a loan please.

A: Certainly, I'll just take down some details. Can I have your name please?

B: It's Whitton. John Whitton.

A: How do you spell your last name?

B: It's W-H-I-T-T-O-N.

A: OK, and your address?

B: 17 Market Street.

A: Thank you, and your phone number?

B: Home, or office?

A: Both please.

B: OK, my home number is 4583298, and my office number is 3849590, no, sorry, it's 950.

A: OK, 3849950, and your date of birth?

B: May 14th, 1979.

A: What is your occupation?

B: I work in IT.

A: How about your salary?

B: I earn 2,000 pounds a month, so my annual salary is 24,000.

A: May I know are you married?

B: Yes, I am.

A: What does your wife do?

B: She's a nurse.

A: And her salary?

B: Her monthly salary is 1,000 pounds.

A: I see, the last question, why do you want the loan?

B: Because I plan to buy a new car.

A: All right then, Mr. Whitton. It will take about one week to process your application.

B: Great, thank you, bye.

A: Good bye, Mr. Whitton.

Example 3

Questions 1-10

Policeman: Good morning! Police station, what can I do for you?

Anna Grieg: Yes, I'd like to report a burglar.

Policeman: I am sorry to hear that. Would you mind if I take down some details?

Anna Grieg: No, please.

Policeman: Well, first of all. What's your name?

Anna Grieg: Anna Grieg.

Policeman: How do you spell them please?

Anna Grieg: Anna is A-N-N-A. Grieg. G-R-I-E-G.

Policeman: OK, may I know how old are you?

Anna Grieg: Yes, I was born on the 15th of the third month 1980.

Policeman: And your address?

Anna Grieg: It's 34 Ellendale. That's E-L-L-E-N-D-A-L-E.

Policeman: And your postcode?

Anna Grieg: That's M528T.

Policeman: OK, are you local?

Anna Grieg: Well, I was born in Singapore, but I am studying for a degree in Oxford University.

Policeman: I see. Is this the first time that you got broken in?

Anna Grieg: Yes, I have been living here for about one year already. It is quite good actually, but I am kind of scared today.

Policeman: May I know how many people do you live with?

Anna Grieg: Just myself.

Policeman: Okay, where do you think the burglar came into your apartment?

Anna Grieg: Well, I am not sure, but I guess it is from the back door, because the front door is locked undamaged, and the windows are not broken.

Policeman: I see, have you noticed what are missing?

Anna Grieg: Well, I am not sure, because my room is in a mess, and the first thing came to my mind is to call you. Let me check it now, yes my computer, I remember that I put it on my desk.

Policeman: OK, do you still remember the serial number of your computer?

Anna Grieg: Yes, I think I have written it down somewhere. Let me find it. Mm. Yes, here it is, it is QS41885377020.

Policeman: OK, is there anything else missing?

Anna Grieg: Yes, I haven't seen my purse.

Policeman: What' in the purse, and can you describe it a little bit?

Anna Grieg: Yes, there is some cash, although I do not remember how much exactly, several hundred maybe. And it is a cloth one of silver color.

Policeman: OK, I have taken it down. Is there anything else?

Anna Grieg: I think that's what I know now.

Policeman: You can always call us if you find anything else missing.

Anna Grieg: Yes, thank you, I will do.

第二周　星期二　多选题

Example 1

Questions 1-4

*Choose the correct letter **A**, **B**, **C** or **D**.*

Janice: Hi, George.

George: Hi, Janice. How are you? I haven't seen you for a while. Do you still live on campus?

Janice: No, I've moved to Oxford Street last week. Actually, I was thinking of going to see you because I'm going to have a party.

George: Oh, sounds great. When is it?

Janice: Well, I was going to hold it on Friday, but Sarah has to work that day. So how about the day after to you?

George: Any day will be fine with me, except Sunday, because I have to get up early the next day.

Janice: OK, Saturday it is then.

George: What time exactly?

Janice: Well, I think I can get dinner ready for about 7 o'clock, so I'm asking people to arrive at 6:30. Is that OK with you?

George: Sure, but I'll be there at a quarter to seven. By the way, shall I bring anything? Maybe something to drink?

Janice: Well, Sarah is bringing some juice, and I have enough beer at home, maybe a bottle of wine, just in case somebody might want to drink, and some cookies if possible.

George: OK, no problem, actually I am on my way to the supermarket, so I can buy some today. How about music? Shall I take some of my instruments so that people can play some music?

Janice: Great, thank you.

George: What would you think I should bring, guitar, flute, piano?

Janice: Well, no, don't bother. I think piano is just too heavy, and I do not think they can play flute well. Just take your guitar. We can sing with it.

George: OK, I will do, so see you Saturday.

Janice: Yes, see you Saturday. Have a nice day.

George: Thank you. Have a nice day.

Example 2

Questions 1-5

*Choose the correct letter **A**, **B** or **C**.*

Hans: Have you decided what to do your research project on yet?

Lily: I thought I'd look at different teaching approaches and see what are more efficient.

Hans: Oh, really. That's quite similar to what I want to do. How are you going to do your research? Are you going to interview teachers, observe classes, or what?

Lily: Neither, I thought I'd use a questionnaire approach. But I am not sure now, would you give me some suggestions?

Hans: Sure, but do you still remember the book we discussed last week, which says that the questionnaires are not very good to do research?

Lily: Yes, I agree, but I need several months if I take the interview approach, you know, I want to get ideas from more people. And I will only use them to get students' opinion.

Hans: I see, would you collect the teachers' ideas?

Lily: Sure, I think I should talk to them, because they can tell me more accurately how they think of different teaching approaches.

Hans: That's true; would you also observe their classes?

Lily: Yes, actually I have observed two classes already, but by talking to the teachers, I realized that if I sit in a class the students would act more differently than they normally act, and this would not give me very reliable information.

Hans: Oh, yes, then I need to rethink about my research as well.

Lily: What are you going to do your research on then, you said it is very similar to mine.

Hans: Yes, I am also thinking of looking at teaching methodology, but instead of looking at all the approaches, I thought I'd just look at one specific approach.

Lily: Oh, really, that's interesting, which method are you looking at?

Hans: Group work, you know, I think the group work is not a good method to teach.

Lily: Why do you think so? That is one of the most commonly used method in teaching.

Hans: Well, take group assignments for example, very often, only part of the students are working, or sometimes, the group members will take turns to finish the tasks given by teachers.

Lily: Yes, that's true, I have found that. And that would defeat the purpose of group work then.

Hans: Yes, that is why I want to look at it. Because students are supposed to cooperate and communicate in group work, if they take turns to finish different tasks, it is of the same function of individual work then.

Lily: Yes, that's a very interesting point, but how are you going to do your research?

Hans: Well, I thought I need to interview both teachers and students. I need to get to know how they think of this method, and maybe I would observe some classes. Would you think it is necessary?

Lily: Yes, I definitely think you need to go to the class, to see if the students are doing as expected in the class.

Hans: Great, I will do that, thank you very much. I think I will go back and rethink about my research.

Lily: Good, see you then.

Hans: See you.

Example 3

Questions 1-7

*Choose the correct letter **A**, **B** or **C**.*

Tom: Hi, May, tomorrow is Friday, are you ready for tomorrow's presentation about a mammal?

May: Well, not really, but I have been to the library yesterday, and have taken down many notes, so I just need to sort it out now.

Tom: Oh really, what are you looking at?

May: Chimpanzees.

Tom: What? Chimps, how did you think of that?

May: Well, I have watched a documentary about chimps before, and I happened to see many books about it yesterday in the library, and find out it is a very interesting topic now.

Tom: Really, I don't know much about it. What have you found already?

May: Well, a lot. Do you know that Chimpanzees make tools and use them to acquire foods and for social displays; they have sophisticated hunting strategies requiring cooperation, influence and rank; and they are status-conscious, manipulative and capable of deception; also they can learn to use symbols and understand aspects of human language including some relational syntax, concepts of number and numerical sequence and they are capable of spontaneous planning for a future state or event.

Tom: Unbelievable. I know chimps are clever animals, but I didn't expect that much. Now I am interested. Tell me some more please.

May: No problem, for example, the tools they use, according to some recent research, the chimpanzee stone tool use dates to at least 4,300 years ago. They dig into termite mounds with a large stick tool, and then using a small stick that has been altered to "fish" the termites out. Once the termites climb on the stick, they would lick and eat them all.

Tom: It is said that chimps can break nuts with stones, is that true?

May: Oh, yes, most definitely. And they have spiritual life even.

Tom: Are you kidding, how is that possible?

May: Well, yes, I have some evidence recorded here. Say they display mourning, dance in the rain, and appreciate the natural beauty such as a sunset over a lake; they may even show empathy toward other species such as feeding turtles.

Tom: Wow, that's amazing. I have never heard about it before.

May: Yes, me either. I have only got this yesterday.

Tom: Is that all your presentation?

May: No, I will also talk about their language.

Tom: Their language, they can't speak, can they?

May: Well, they can, they communicate in a manner similar to human non-verbal communication, using vocalizations, hand gestures, and facial expressions, and so on.

Tom: But I thought scientists have long been fascinated with the studies of language, believing it to be a unique human cognitive ability.

May: Yes. To test this hypothesis, scientists have attempted to teach human language to several species of great apes. One early attempt by Allen and Beatrice Gardner in the 1960s involved spending 51 months teaching American Sign Language to a chimpanzee named Washoe. The Gardners reported that Washoe learned 151 signs, and that she had spontaneously taught them to other chimpanzees. Over a longer period of time, Washoe learned over 800 signs.

Tom: So language is not human specific then?

May: Actually, there is ongoing debate among some scientists, notably Noam Chomsky and David Premack, about non-human great apes' ability to learn language. Since the early reports on Washoe, numerous other studies have been conducted with varying levels of success.

Tom: Wow, you have done enough study; I think your presentation is going to be very interesting.

May: I hope so, and I think I'd better go and get started.

Tom: Yes, me too. I think I have to go to the library as well.

May: Yes, good luck to you.

Tom: Thank you, good bye.

第二周　星期三　填图题

Example 1

You will hear a tour guide talking to a group of people at the new town library.

OK, everyone. Now we are standing in front of the town library, which has been built only three years ago, but it attracted many visitors because of its plentiful resources.

Before we enter, I would like to tell you a bit about the way the library is organized, so that you may have a global view of the library. In general, the library is an oval one, with two entrances, one in the front and one on its side.

When we enter, we can first see the chief librarian's office on our left, opposite to which, there is an information desk next to the catalogue, which still keeps the very traditional catalogue, although there is a computer index system that readers can use in almost every room.

If we go in, there is a huge reading hall available for all the readers, which means anybody can read there, and you do not have to get a library card if you do not read books borrowed in the library. Very often, many people come to read their own books, because it is quiet and it is totally free.

On both sides of the reading hall, there is a small room with plenty of reference books, and in the other room, readers can have up-to-date periodicals such as newspapers and magazines and this room also has a photocopier in case you want to copy any of the articles. If you carry straight on you'll come into a large room and this is the seminar room, and that can be booked for meetings or talks, and next door to that is the children's library, which has a good collection of stories and picture books for the under elevens. Then there's a large room to the right of the newspaper area – that's the multimedia collection, where you can borrow videos and DVDs and so on, and we also have CD-ROMs you can borrow to use on your computer at home. It was originally the art collection but that's been moved to another building. Then, we are going out of the library from its side gate there. OK, now does anyone have any questions? If no, I wish you have a nice time in it, please make sure we are going to meet in front of the side gate in one hour.

Example 2

You are now going to listen to someone introduce the campus of a university.

First you have some time to look at the questions 1-10.

Now listen to the introduction and match the places with the numbers.

Good afternoon, everyone. Welcome to the annual conference. Since you are going to stay here for about one week, I think you might be using many facilities in the university, so I would like to give a brief introduction about the campus arrangements, so that you can get an idea where is where.

Now, when you enter, I think you have realized that this is our front gate, and in front of us, is where the administrative staff work, and on our right hand, it is the conference building. I think you will be staying in it a lot, because most of the conference sessions will be taken inside. Opposite the conference building is one of our teaching buildings, and there is a bigger one behind it, which is the main teaching building. But now, I would like to walk you around from the right side. If we go deep in, we can see a café, which is open most of the time, so you can go in and have some coffee whenever you fancy. In front of the café is a big garden, in which there are plenty of flowers, and there are some benches in the path, you may go in and enjoy the flowers there. On the opposite of the garden, we will see the main teaching building I have mentioned just now, and the canteen building, in the building you can have food of all kinds. The Chinese and Italian food on the second floor is especially good. You must go and have a try.

However, walking out of the canteen, we cannot go directly further. We have to come to the garden, and walk through a very small gate behind the garden, and go to the library and dormitory buildings. The library is in the far south, and there is a huge collection of books, you might go and read some inside, since you do not stay here long, so you don't have to bother to have a card.

By the way, in case some of you might be sporty, I am glad to tell you there is a huge playground if you go through the lane in front of the dormitory. There are all kinds of facilities available, such as football field, basketball and tennis court. On the north side of the playground is our side gate, from where you can go to a big avenue, which is very busy, if you want to go shopping, there is the right place for you.

So that's pretty much about the campus. I hope I have given you a general conception about the arrangement, but do not worry if you are still not clear, because we have a lot of signs around, you would not be lost.

Anybody has any questions for me? Good, I would wish you have a good and rewarding week in this university.

第二周 星期四 完成句子

Example 1

Questions 1-10

Complete the sentences below.

Write ***NO MORE THAN TWO WORDS*** *for each answer.*

Teacher: Good morning. Happy Kids Center, how may I help you?

Parent: Yes, I'd like to enquire a course for my son.

Teacher: No problem, may I know how old your son is?

Parent: He will be 4 years old next birthday. Is there a course for him now? I take care of him myself, but I think he needs to be with other children for sometime every day.

Teacher: I see, many parents send their children here because of this. We have courses for kids from 3 months old to 5 years old.

Parent: Oh, really, that's great. So what do you recommend?

Teacher: Well, it seems that you have some time. Would you want to be involved in the course?

Parent: Sure, if that's possible.

Teacher: Great, there is a cooperative course run by parents. I think you might be interested in.

Parent: That sounds great. Can you please explain it a bit more?

Teacher: Well, actually, it is a kind of survival course that we think is good to every child. The parents can take part in it with the kids.

Parent: Do you think my son is old enough for that?

Teacher: Don't worry, actually it is a course for mixed aged kids. In a sense, being with kids of different ages will help the kids to develop their social skills, and there are many parents doing the courses with the kids, so it is very safe.

Parent: I see, but before we start the course, is there anything we need to prepare?

Teacher: Well, yes, all the parents who attend will have to get the training courses, because there are some dos and don'ts parents need to bear in mind.

Parent: I see, that's no problem with me. Anything else?

Teacher: Yes, do you live afar?

Parent: Well, not really, but why?

Teacher: You know, we often find kids too shy in the course, so if possible, I suggest you take your son and visit the center for several times before he attends the course, so that he can get familiar with the environment and will be more confident in the course.

Parent: I see, that's very helpful. Thank you, I will do that.

Teacher: Good, is there anything else you want to know?

Parent: Yes, can you please tell me how much the course is?

Teacher: Sure, the course is about 3 three months long. For each month, you will have to pay $400.

Parent: I see, but if I go with my son, do I have to pay for the course?

Teacher: Not really, but you do need to pay for some materials, which is about $50, so in your case, you need to pay for $450.

Parent: OK, when can we start then?

Teacher: Well, today is the twentieth; we start at the first Monday of every month. But you need to take register here at the center before that.

Parent: OK, I see. Can I come anytime?

Teacher: Well, yes, but you'd better come on weekdays and we close at 6:30 p.m. every day.

Parent: OK, I got it. I think I will come next Thursday.

Teacher: OK, see you Thursday, then.

Parent: Thank you very much, see you Thursday.

Teacher: You are welcome.

Example 2

Questions 1-8

Listen to the following telephone conversation between a hotel receptionist and a person trying to make a booking. The line is bad but the receptionist has the telephone skills to deal with this problem.

Complete the sentences below.

*Write **NO MORE THAN TWO WORDS** for each answer.*

CONFIRMING A HOTEL BOOKING

Receptionist: Good afternoon. Grand Hotel, how may I help you?

Customer: I'm ringing to confirm a booking I made three days ago. I was expecting a confirming call, but I haven't received anything.

Receptionist: I'm sorry the line is rather bad. Would you mind repeating that, please?

Customer: Yes, I made a reservation on your website under the name of Tilts. George Tilts.

Receptionist: Could you spell your surname for me, please?

Customer: Yes, that's T-I-L-T-S.

Receptionist: And when was the reservation for?

Customer: June 21st to the 25th.

Receptionist: Sorry, did you say the 23rd?

Customer: No, the 21st.

Receptionist: Let me just check if we have your details on the system. Ah... yes, here we are.

Customer: I put down one double and one single room, but I wonder if I could change that.

Receptionist: I'm terribly sorry I didn't quite catch that. Would you mind speaking up a little?

Customer: Yes, I wanted to change the number of rooms. Is it possible to have two doubles instead of a single and a double?

Receptionist: Let's see...oh hold on a moment. I've got someone on the other line. *(Speaks to other customer)* yes, yeah...would you mind if I rang you back? I'm just dealing with a reservation. Thanks.

Customer: Sorry?

Receptionist: Yes, sorry about that Mr. Tilts. I'm just getting your booking details up now. Yes, we do have another double available for those nights. Was there anything else?

Customer: Well, I wanted to know if you did vegetarian food for the evening meal. It wasn't clear from the website.

Receptionist: Yes, we do, but by prior arrangement. But now you've requested it, I'll put that down in the booking. How many people was that for?

Customer: Just myself.

Receptionist: Very good. Anything else?

Customer: Well, we've got a very early return flight on the 26th, seven o'clock, so we'll need an alarm call at about 5:30, I should think.

Receptionist: No problem, sir. I'll arrange that now. Was that all?

Customer: I think so.

Receptionist: So you'd like two double rooms for the nights of the 21st to the 25th June inclusive, vegetarian provision for one and an early morning call on your departure. Is that correct?

Customer: That's right.

Receptionist: If we can help you with anything else, just give us a ring. We look forward to seeing you in June.

Example 3

Waitress: Hello, Global Style Restaurant.

Hans: Hello, do you do group bookings?

Waitress: Yes, we do. How can I help you?

Hans: Well, I'd like to book a table for between 15 and 20, but I am not sure the exact number now.

Waitress: When is it for?

Hans: A week on Saturday.

Waitress: The 9th of October?

Hans: Yes, exactly.

Waitress: OK, well, usually we offer a set menu for groups up to 25 people. If you want, you can order a private room, but it usually works out more expensive and obviously if everybody orders different food, then it can take us a lot longer to prepare. And particularly on a Saturday as we're usually pretty busy.

Hans: So would you recommend the set menu?

Waitress: Well, it's up to you, but it's a good option and you get to try different types of food.

Hans: That's good. We have a couple of vegetarians in the group, some meat eaters, one person who needs gluten-free and another who is allergic to peanuts. That wouldn't be a problem, would it?

Waitress: That's not a problem. We cater for all dietary requirements. We offer several different menus and you can choose which one you prefer. Our basic menu costs £28 per person. We do it for a minimum of 4 people, as with all our menus. That's Menu A. Then they each go up in price depending on which one you order. Menu B is £35 per person. Menu G is £38 per person and Menu J is £45 per person.

Hans: And how do the menus differ?

Waitress: Well, all our set menus include a variety of food—some Asian style, some Mediterranean, some Latin American and some British food.

Hans: And can you mix all types of food in each menu?

Waitress: Yes, that's right. Basically you get a selection of starters for the whole table, for example in Menu A, you get a goat's cheese salad, onion bhajis and guacamole. With Menu J, you get spare ribs, king prawns, hummus and pitta bread and a selection of salads. You get more options with the more expensive menus. Also with the cheaper menus, you get house wine, it works out at one bottle between 2 people. With the other menus, you have a choice of wine; with Menu J, you can also have cava.

Hans: What about the main courses?

Waitress: You have a choice of 3 options. All menus also include a dessert and coffee.

Hans: Right, I see. Could I pop by and pick up some menus to have a look at?

Waitress: Of course. Or I could e-mail them to you, if you want, to save you the trouble.

Hans: That'd be great.

Waitress: So, what's your name?

Hans: My name is Hans Delly — that's H-A-N-S-D-E-L-L-Y.

Waitress: OK, Hans. And your e-mail?

Hans: That's hans8005@gmail.com. And my phone number is 05725 693563.

Waitress: All right, so would you like to make a temporary reservation?

Hans: Can I do that?

Waitress: Yeah. I can pencil you in for — how many people did you say?

Hans: Well, I'm not sure, between 15 and 20.

Waitress: OK, that's fine. You can confirm numbers and which menus you want a couple of days before.

Hans: OK, that's great.

Waitress: And I'll send you the e-mail with the menus right now.

Hans: OK, thanks a lot.

Waitress: No problem. If there's anything else you need, you can get in touch and ask for me. My name's Barr.

Hans: Great. Thanks, Barr. Bye.

Waitress: Bye.

第二周　星期五　补全题

Example 1

Good morning, listeners. Today I would like to talk about the primary education in UK. But, before that, I would like you to take a look at the general conduct on primary education in the world.

Primary or elementary education is the first years of formal, structured education that occurs during childhood. In most Western countries, it is compulsory for children to receive primary education.

Primary education generally begins when children are four to seven years of age. The division between primary and secondary education is somewhat arbitrary, but it generally occurs at about twelve years of age; some educational systems have separate middle schools for that period. Primary and secondary education together are sometimes (in particular, in Canada and the United States) referred to as " K-12" education (K is for kindergarten, 12 is for twelfth grade).

Typically, primary education is provided in schools , where (in the absence of parental movement or other intervening factors) the child will stay, in steadily advancing classes, until they complete it and move on to secondary schooling. Children are usually placed in classes with one teacher who will be primarily responsible for their education and welfare for that year. This teacher may be assisted to varying degrees by specialist teachers in certain subject areas, often music or physical education. The continuity with a single teacher and the opportunity to build up a close relationship with the class is a notable feature of the primary education system. Over the past few decades, schools have been testing various arrangements which break from the one-teacher, one-class mold.

The major goals of primary education are achieving basic literacy and numeracy amongst all their students, as well as establishing foundations in science, geography, history and other social sciences. The relative priority of various areas, and the methods used to teach them, are an area of considerable political debate.

Traditionally, various forms of corporal punishment were an integral part of early education in the UK. This practice has now been outlawed in the UK.

Example 2

When buying a house, consumers have to deal with estate agents, solicitors, surveyors, builders, lenders and others. When they want to buy a property, the chances are people won't have tens of thousands of pounds stashed under the bed so they need to approach a mortgage lender to help with the purchase. Mortgage lenders are able to lend a great deal more money on the purchase of a house as opposed to a purchase for a car or a holiday because property tends to hold its value or increases in value over time. This ensures that they will probably be able to recoup much of the loan if anything goes wrong. Needless to say, this doesn't mean that they don't make a great deal of money out of mortgages. Generally over the period of a mortgage the borrower will pay back nearly three times as much as they borrowed!

Until recently nearly all home buyers would have used a Building Society to provide them with a mortgage but the industry has undergone something of a shake-up in recent years with many Societies converting to or being taken over by Banks. Building Societies offered better interest rates on mortgages as they were owned by the people who saved or borrowed from them known as members. This meant that whereas banks had to maximise their profits to allow for payments to be made to shareholders the Building Societies could be more competitive as they were not profit driven. Building Societies can still work out cheaper but many banks now offer competitive rates and the market has been joined by other lenders such as Internet or telephone lenders who can compete by keeping down the overheads incurred by having a high street presence. Although many borrowers still like to visit a branch to discuss their requirements a significant amount are happy to conduct their business over the phone or on the web.

Example 3

The first man to combine the steam engines and wagon-ways was Richard Trevithick. An engineer, he designed a steam engine that could run on wheels in 1803. In 1804, his engine pulled wagons carrying 18 tonnes of iron ore and 70 men for five miles (14km) in South Wales, but it was so heavy that the track broke when it reached five miles per hour (8kph).

The rail transport system in Great Britain developed during the 19th century. Britain's railways were initially owned by four companies, then during WWII they were the railways were taken into state control and they were nationalised in 1947. It wasn't until 1996 that they were privatized again!

Today there are 25 train operators who run the services. One infrastructure company—Network Rail. Three rolling stock companies. And all sorts of companies who do maintenance work on the 13,000 miles of track. There are also a number of government organisations like the Strategic Rail Authority and the Health and Safety Executive which are involved in running the railways, making the whole structure extremely complicated.

Broken tracks, leaves or the wrong type of snow on the line and trains past their sell by date are a feature of rail travel in the UK nowadays where, according to statistics, only two out of ten British trains are late, the main problem is they always seem to be my trains! If you have a problem when travelling by train in Britain there is a very good network called the Rail Passenger Council which deals with complaints and will also give a lot of advice on problems.

第二周　星期六　配对题

Example 1

Questions 1-4

You will hear a woman talking to a travel agent.

Which hotel matches each description?

*Choose your answers from the box and write the correct letter, **A-D**, next to questions 1-4.*

Travel agent: New Age Tours, good morning. Can I help you?

Woman: Yes, I have booked a trip with you to the south. I was wondering if I can book a hotel through you.

Travel agent: Sure, may I know what kind of accommodation you are looking for?

Woman: Well, I am not sure, maybe a four star hotel if possible. Do you have something about the possibilities?

Travel agent: OK, right, well, there are four hotels that might interest you. Were you wanting a city centre location, or would you be interested in something a bit further out?

Woman: Well, I do plan to hire a car there, so I don't mind going for either.

Travel agent: Well, there are three central hotels in the range you're looking for — there's Hilton House and the Emperor's. They're both at the city center, but if you've got your own transport you might be interested in the Big Apple — that's out in the country, about twenty kilometres away, very peaceful. Then there's the Skypass hotel — it is in town but not in the centre — they're out on the airport road.

Woman: Mmm. That might be a bit far out actually. OK, now the other two you mentioned, in the city centre. Can you tell me a bit about them?

Travel agent: Well, they're both popular hotels. If you want something with a bit of character, Hilton House is quite unusual—it's a very old building that was originally a large private house, it was completely refurbished—they took their first guests just a few months ago but it's already got an excellent reputation. That's a four star hotel. Or there's the Emperor's, which is a much more modern building. That also has its own gym and it also has Internet connection and meetings rooms—it's used for conferences and corporate events as well as private guests. That's four star as well.

Woman: Does it have a swimming pool as well as a gym?

Travel agent: No—the Big Apple has an outdoor pool, which is lovely in the summer, but the only hotel with an indoor pool is the Skypass Hotel. It doesn't have a gym though. They are planning to build a swimming pool and a fitness centre, but it's not finished yet.

Woman: Well, I think I'll probably go for one of the city centre hotels.

Travel agent: OK, so...

Example 2

You will hear a Telecommunication Studies student talking to his tutor about optional courses for the next semester.

Professor Green: Hello, George. I haven't seen you for a while. What do you want to talk about today?

George: Well, yes. I really want to talk about my optional courses next semester, you know, it is almost about the deadline now.

Professor Green: Yes, what do you have in mind now?

George: Well, you know, I'd like to do all five courses, but we can only do two, right?

Professor Green: Yes, the choice depends on your major to some extent. How do you call your major exactly?

George: It's telecommunication.

Professor Green: So the mass media will be a very good choice then. It is quite important for your major, and it is a very popular course.

George: Mmm. Well, that was interesting, but I've decided I'd rather do something completely new. You know, mass media is quite close to some of the courses I have taken, and there's a Children's Studies option, isn't there?

Professor Green: Yes, "Children and Education", it aims to look at the influence of modern technology on children's education.

George: That sounds interesting, but I'm not sure I do actually.

Professor Green: Well, it might still be useful to give you an idea of the issues involved. It's taught by Dr. Stevenson.

George: Oh, really? I'll sign up for that, then. What about the option on Western Culture?

Professor Green: That addresses the historical debate on the place of culture in the major western developed countries.

George: That sounds great, but only western culture?

Professor Green: Do I get the message you're interested in some other parts of the world?

George: Well, it's just we seem to have done quite a lot this semester ... anyway I'll think about that one.

Professor Green: If you're interested in a course focusing on current issues there's the option on overseas students' identity — you know, many overseas students are not really sure of their identity since they stayed in another country for years.

George: Oh? That sounds interesting. Can you tell me who runs it?

Professor Green: Well, it's normally Dr. Speary, but he's in Japan next semester, so I'm not sure who'll be running it. It should be decided by next week though.

George: Right, well, I might wait until then to decide … And the last option is Introduction to Digitalization, isn't it? I'm quite interested in that too—I was talking to one of the second year students, and she said it was really useful.

Professor Green: Yes, but in fact in your major, you'll have covered a lot of that already in digital products, so that might be less useful than some of the others.

George: Oh, I'll forget about that one, then.

Professor Green: Now while you're here, we could also discuss how you're getting on with your Remote Control assignment …

第二周　星期日　简答题

Example 1

Questions 1-7

Answer the following questions.

Write ***NO MORE THAN THREE WORDS*** *for each answer.*

Manager: Good morning, customer service, what can I do for you?

Customer: Yes, may I speak to the manager please?

Manager: This is the manager speaking.

Customer: Great, I bought one computer from your company, but it's stopped working.

Manager: I am sorry for that, but to be more specific, what model is your computer?

Customer: The model number is T450.

Manager: OK, when did you buy it?

Customer: Last month. I can't remember the exact date.

Manager: That's OK. Where did you buy it?

Customer: From your department store on Sutton Road.

Manager: Sutton Road store, I see. And how much did you pay for it?

Customer: Originally it was $600, but I bought it in a sale for $400.

Manager: OK, can you tell me what the problem is?

Customer: Well, I don't know really. It just suddenly stopped working.

Manager: Have you checked the battery? Do you think it is properly installed?

Customer: Of course I did. That is the first thing I checked.

Manager: Did you contact the store where you bought it?

Customer: Yes, I did, but the manager said that because I bought it in a sale, he refused to change it, although it is still in the warranty time.

.I see. Do you know his name?

Customer: Yes, his name is Peter Wisborough.

Manager: When did you contact him?

Customer: Well, my computer stopped working last Monday, and I called him the day after.

Manager: OK, I tell you what I'll do. I'll contact Mr. Wisborough myself and tell him to replace your computer. So just call into the store anytime after tomorrow, and they will replace it for you.

Customer: Thank you very much.

Manager: You are welcome, and you can always contact me if you have any problem with your computer.

Customer: That's great, thanks, bye.

Manager: Bye.

Example 2

Questions 1-10

Answer the following questions.
*Write **NO MORE THAN THREE WORDS** for each answer.*
A dialogue between Jack and Jane who are planning an evening out.

Jack: Hi Jane!

Jane: Hi Jack!

Jack: How's everything?

Jane: Oh, pretty good.

Jack: Are we still on for this evening? Want to do something?

Jane: Yeah, how about going to the concert?

Jack: Oh no, I really hate the crowds. What about a drink or something to eat?

Jane: OK, how about going to the Cantonese food restaurant in my area?

Jack: Oh, I'm teaching until quite late ... How about something more ... perhaps in the city center, so it will not be too far for both of us.

Jane: Allright, well, is there any good restaurant around?

Jack: Well, what sort of food do you fancy? Cantonese only?

Jane: Well, not really, I like Japanese food as well, maybe some sashimi.

Jack: Sure ... a bit expensive though.

Jane: Well ... let's ... well ... a cheaper one then.

Jack: I tell you what, I saw one advertised the other day in the Bristol Square; it's called Eastern Café.

Jane: Wow ... it sounds interesting!

Jack: It says that there is a big buffet so maybe you can get the sashimi and stuff.

Jane: Yeah, good idea.

Jack: OK, there it is. When shall we meet?

Jane: Well, how late are you going to be then?

Jack: Yes, I finish at 9:30 pm, so ...

Jane: I see ... 9:30 pm? Let's meet, say, 9:40 pm?

Jack: OK. Whereabouts?

Jane: I see ... Shall we meet at the bus stop, right outside the campus?

Jack: OK, that'd be good, that'd be good. So 9:40 pm by the bus stop.

Jane: OK.

Jack: OK, see you then.

Jane: Hey, hang on Jack. Do we have to book? It's meant to be busy.

Jack: Oh, hang on ... yeah, that might be a good idea. Umm, can you do that?

Jane: Yes, I can do that since you're teaching.

Jack: I'll just get the number, hang on, let me have a look…it's called Eastern café , 3655 9889. OK. It sounds quite interesting. It says here they've got 6 open kitchens, 400 seats and a 12 seat "cool room" with flat screen TVs and stuff.

Jane: Well, we can watch the football game tonight.

Jack: Yeah, and different types of food; Mongolian food, Indian food, Australian ...

Jane: It's a good mix!

Jack: Anyway Jane, I've got to go now. I'll see you tonight.

Jane: OK, 9:45pm, a table for 2.

Jack: OK, see you later. Bye!

Example 3

Listen to this interview with 65-year-old Brain Bullough. He retired last year after 15 years employment with a car manufacturer.

Interviewer: Brain, how does it feel to be retired?

Brain: Well, you know, not so bad …

Interviewer: How have you been spending your time?

Brain: Like everyone I've been spending more time with my family, I've also travelled a bit, you know offseason when everywhere's less crowded and hotels cost less …

Interviewer: Great …

Brain: You know I haven't stopped work completely …

Interviewer: Yes, could you tell us more about this?

Brain: I'm on a scheme that's called "phased retirement". I had a 6 months break from work, after that I could apply for project work with the company I used to work for.

Interviewer: How does the scheme work?

Brain: Well, it's a trial at the moment. Instead of hiring temporary staff the company advertises posts on its website that retired employees like myself can access.

Interviewer: What sort of work's advertised?

Brain: Well, all sorts of things really. Admin work—there's lots of that, then there's more specialised work, the sort of thing I can do. Some of the projects can be long term say for 5 or 6 months, others can just be a couple of days or weeks. Again the number of hours included in a project can vary. I can decide, more or less, when to work, you know I manage my own time —it's great, it's very flexible and I do it all from home …

Interviewer: I can see it's good for you. What does your company get out of this?

Brain: Well, I still have all my old contacts at work, so I know who to contact to get something done — a temp brought in from outside doesn't have this knowledge so it takes them longer to get a job done. The company gets flexibility too. Once the job's over that's it, I'm not on their books any more. No training's required either, not yet anyway, so there are savings there too .

Interviewer: Do you have to commit yourself to a certain number of hours a week?

Brain: Not at all. I can do as much or as little as I like …

Interviewer: How about keeping your skills up to date?

Brain: I've got access to a lot of online courses, you know, e-learning—if I'm not sure of something I have a look there …

Interviewer: Do you pay tax?

Brain: Sure. The tax situation's a bit complicated at the moment with this being a trial but I pay tax on what I earn, yes, unfortunately …

Interviewer: And those holidays …?

Brain: Well, you know. I work in the summer when most people are on holiday—then it's time for my holiday. Holidays, sure. we go to Europe three or four times a year …

第三周　常考场景精练

第三周　星期一　租房

场景一：电话找房

You are now going to listen to someone enquiring about an apartment. First, you have some time to look at questions 1-5.

30 second pause

Listen to the conversation and answer questions 1-5.

Man: Hi, I'm calling to see if the apartment you have advertised in last evening's newspaper is still available.

Landlady: Yes, it is.

Man: Great, may I ask several questions?

Landlady: Sure, what would you like to know?

Man: Where is the apartment located?

Landlady: It's on the tenth floor of a high-rise apartment block, and it is about ten minutes walk from the subway station close to the Bath University.

Man: Great, but is it OK if I keep pets?

Landlady: What type of pets? I hope it's not a big dog.

Man: Oh, no. It's a cat.

Landlady: That shouldn't be a problem.

Man: Ah, that's good. So how big is the apartment?

Landlady: Two bedrooms. Plus a kitchen , a bathroom and a balcony.

Man: And what about a living room?

Landlady: Oh, yes, sorry, I forgot about that. There's also a living room. It's quite small though.

Man: That's good. And are all the rooms heated?

Landlady: Yes, There's heating in each room.

Man: Now about the facilities.

Landlady: Well, it's half furnished. There's a couch and a table in the main lounge, and two beds, one in each bedroom, as well as wardrobes. There's a TV, but there is no microwave oven, I am afraid.

You now have some time to look at questions 6-10.

30 second pause

Now listen to the rest of the conversation and answer questions 6-10.

Man: So how much is the rent?

Landlady: £350 a month.

Man: What does it include?

Landlady: That includes ground rent, though, the maintenance fee and the heating. You have to pay for the water and electricity yourself.

Man: Oh, I see. And how long would the contract be for?

Landlady: That's mainly up to you. We prefer one year contract though.

Man: Actually, I was thinking about maybe two years if possible, because I will have to stay there long.

Landlady: Two years? That's even better.

Man: Would you mind telling me why you want to rent the place out?

Landlady: Not at all. I'm going to work overseas. In fact I'll be teaching at the University of Melbourne.

Man: University of Melbourne? That's funny. I am working there, but I will work in the University of Bath.

Landlady: Oh, really, do you happen to have an apartment?

Man: Actually I do. It's about the same size of yours.

Landlady: I have an idea. Can we just exchange our apartment? and neither of us needs to pay the rent.

Man: That's a marvelous idea; maybe we should meet and talk about the details.

Landlady: Why not come to my apartment? and you can take a look at it.

Man: That's great. When is it convenient?

Landlady: Any time, how about now?

Man: Great, I will come now. What's the address?

Landlady: It's 34 Bath Road.

Man: Great, see you soon.

Landlady: See you.

场景二：向朋友咨询租房

You will hear a telephone conversation between an Indian student, Mohamod, and an American lady, Shirley, about renting an apartment. First, look at questions 1-6.

20 second pause

Now listen to the conversation and answer the questions.

Shirley: Good morning. Who's speaking?

Mohamod: Good morning. This is Mohamod, you remember me, we met in a summer camp in India last year.

Shirley: Yes, I do. How are you?

Mohamd: I am OK. I am calling to ask a favor of you?

Shirley: Yes, what can I do for you?

Mohamod: You know, I have just been here in America yesterday. I had a job here, so I have to rent an apartment, but I'm not really sure about the best way of going about it. I was wondering if you could help me out. Give me some advice.

Shirley: Yeah. Looking for an apartment is really difficult. Well, there're two ways I could suggest. You could go to a rental agent…

Mohamod: An agent, yeah.

Shirley: …which is a bit expensive. Or the other way is to look in the classified ads in the newspapers.

Mohamod: Newspapers.

Shirley: You could look in either the…*New York Times* is good, or *the Village Voice*.

Mohamod: Are they the best papers?

Shirley: Yeah. I would say *the Village Voice* is fine.

Mohamod: *The Village Voice* is fine. OK. Let me get that down. That's *the Village Voice* and *New York Times*. OK.

Shirley: OK?

Mohamod: Yeah.

Shirley: And, well, I think the most important thing, if you're going to use the newspapers, is to get the papers early and call the places very early because a lot of people are looking for apartments in New York.

Mohamod: OK. And another question I had is, I'm not really sure about where to look, in what area of Manhattan. What do you think would be nice neighborhood?

Shirley: Anywhere on the East Side from 14th to 59th on Street.

Mohamod: Wait a second. That's 14th…

Shirley: 14th.

Mohamod: 14th to…

Shirley: 59th, OK.

Mohamod: 59th, OK.

Shirley: That's a good area. Or you could live in Greenwich Village.

Mohamod: Where's that, exactly?

Shirley: Well, actually, if you're going to Columbia, that might be a little inconvenient for you. But from 14th to 59th on the East Side you could take the subway right up to the Columbia.

Mohamod: OK. That'd be good. And what can I expect to pay? I'm a little bit concerned about the money.

Shirley: About $400 plus utilities…

Mohamod: $400 plus.

Shirley:…for a small but nice apartment.

Mohamod: Actually, that's OK. My company is going to help me pay. They'll pay up to $500 so I'd like to keep it under five hundred.

Shirley: Yeah. You could find one for that.

Mohamod: Well, so then, you think I should use the papers.

Shirley: Yeah, I'd recommend that.

Mohamod: OK. I think that's what I'll do, and I'd like to get busy on this right away.

Garol: OK. Good luck in apartment hunting.

Mohamod: Yeah. Thanks very much.

场景三：与房东谈论租房

You are going to hear a conversation between a landlord and George, who is going to rent an apartment.

First you have some time to look at the questions1-8.

30 second pause

Now listen to the conversation and answer the questions.

Landlord: Well, you've seen the apartment. What do you think?

George: Well, actually. I like the apartment. But I was thinking that if I decide to take it. There are a few things that I'd like to have done.

Landlord: Like what?

George: Well, for example, the locks. I'd like to have the locks changed.

Landlord: OK. I can probably have the locks changed in a day or two.

George: You could. Good. And then, in the kitchen, I noticed that the sink seems to have a bad leak. Could you have somebody take a look at that?

Landlord: OK. I guess I can have someone look at it next week sometime. Probably just needs tightening.

George: And also in the kitchen, on the window next to the refrigerator. I noticed there are a couple of big cracks, and I'm afraid the glass might fall out and then when the winter comes, there might be a lot of draughts. Could you have somebody do something about that?

Landlord: OK. Well, if that turns out to be a problem then I'll ask the "super" and maybe he can take care of it. Can't promise when, though.

George: But you will mention it to him.

Landlord: Yeah, I'll mention it to him.

George: OK, and the only other thing is the paint. I noticed in a lot of the rooms, the paint is pretty dingy. Could you have the place painted?

Landlord: Well, we don't do any of the painting, so you'll have to paint it yourself.

George: If I do paint it myself, would you reimburse me for the paint?

Landlord: No, I don't think so, because sometimes people just want to, you know, paint over what's new paint, so unh-unh.

George: Well, here the paint is not new though.

Landlord: Well, that's all the questions that I have about the place.

Landlord: OK. Well, let me tell you some of the rules that we have. No pets. No loud music after 11 p.m. A month's deposit. A month in advance. Twelve month lease. If you break the lease you lose your deposit.

George: I see. So I have to give you two months rent if I decide to take the place, right?

Landlord: Right. Right.

George: That's a … that'll be $ 860 altogether.

Landlord: Right. And you'll have to pay gas and water.

George: Yeah, OK. I understand that. Well, I think I'd like to take the place.

Landlord: Well, if you could have the locks changed by the end of this week…

Landlord: Yeah.

George:… I can move in early next week.

Landlord: OK. All right. That's OK. Well, then, why don't we go downstairs and sign the papers.

George: Sure.

第三周　星期二　学校

场景一：语言学习

You are going to hear somebody talking about tips on learning foreign language.

First you have some time to look at the questions1-5.

30 second pause

Now listen to the conversation and answer the questions.

Good morning, listeners. Today we are going to talk about some basic tips on how to learn a foreign language.

First of all, spend the time!

By far the most important factor is how much time you are immersed in the language. The more time you spend with the language, the faster you will learn. This means listening, reading, writing, speaking, and studying words and phrases. This does not mean sitting in class looking out the window, nor listening to other students who do not speak well, nor getting explanations in your own language about how the language works. This means spending time enjoyably connected to the language you are learning.

The next tip is to listen and read every day!

Listen wherever you are on your MP3 player. Read what you are listening to. Listen to and read things that you like, things that you can mostly understand, or even partly understand. If you keep listening and reading you will get used to the language. One hour of listening or reading is more effective than many hours of class time.

Next, focus on words and phrases!

Build up your vocabulary, you'll need lots. Start to notice words and how they come together as phrases. Learn these words and phrases through your listening and reading. Read online, using online dictionaries, and make your own vocabulary lists for review. Soon you will run into your new words and phrases elsewhere. Gradually you will be able to use them. Do not worry about how accurately you speak until you have accumulated a plenty of words through listening and reading.

In addition, take responsibility for your own learning!

If you do not want to learn the language, you won't. If you do want to learn the language, take control. Choose content of interest that you want to listen to and read. Seek out the words and phrases that you need to understand your listening and reading. Do not wait for someone else to show you the language, nor to tell you what to do. Discover the language by yourself, like a child growing up. Talk when you feel like it. Write when you feel like it. A teacher cannot teach you to become fluent, but you can learn to become fluent if you want to.

Finally, relax and enjoy yourself!

Do not worry about what you cannot remember, or cannot yet understand, or cannot yet say. It does not matter. You are learning and improving. The language will gradually become clearer in your brain, but this will happen on a schedule that you cannot control. So sit back and enjoy. Just make sure you spend enough time with the language. That is the greatest guarantee of success.

Learning a foreign language is never an easy job. You need to enjoy it. Good luck to your language learning, goodbye now.

场景二：课程咨询

You are going to hear a conversation between two people talking about evening courses.

First you have some time to look at the questions1-6.

30 second pause

Now listen to the conversation and answer the questions.

Receptionist: Good afternoon. King's College. Can I help you?

Caller: Yes, please. I'd like to enquiry about evening courses your college has…

Receptionist: OK…which subjects are you interested in?

Caller: Well, I want to learn a foreign language and some computer skills.

Receptionist: OK. What language are you interested in?

Caller: Actually, I'm not sure. I have to fulfill a language requirement for school, but I haven't really decided what language to study. Um…how many language courses do you provide?

Receptionist: Well, we have foreign language classes from Monday to Thursday, including French, Spanish, German, and Chinese.

Caller: Great. And how much do the courses cost?

Receptionist: Each course costs ￡25.00 per person per term, but if you want to do TWO language courses, there's a 25% discount, but only if you book for two terms.

Caller: Great. Would it be possible for me to book my classes right now?

Receptionist: No, sorry, the computer's down. What I suggest you do is call extension 9664 …no, sorry…9694, after 6.00 p.m. and ask for Mrs. Green.

Caller: Thanks. OK, can we now look at the Computer Skills Courses?

Receptionist: Yes, of course. Computer classes always start in the first week of the month, and the way it works is, we offer one computer class for the entire month. So you might spend one month on Word…another month on Excel, and so on. Classes meet once a week, on Monday afternoons. The next class starts May 8th.

Caller: OK, so for the upcoming month…May…?

Receptionist: May is going to be Word. There are places available and it costs ￡45.00 per person.

Caller: May…Word…￡45.00…OK…

Receptionist: Excel starts in June and that's nearly full-only four slots left. It's ￡55.00.

Caller: OK, Excel…June…only four slots left…got it.

Receptionist: July is Powerpoint. It is ￡60.00 for the month.

Caller: Now, do I call the same number to book a place in one of these classes?

Receptionist: No, you have to call Sarah, her extension 9663.

Caller: OK. Many thanks for all your help.

场景三：图书馆预约书

You are going to listen to someone reserving a library book. First you have some time to look at questions 1-6.

30 second pause

Now listen to the conversation and answer the questions.

Librarian: Good morning, National Library.

Customer: Good morning, I'd like to reserve a book please.

Librarian: Certainly, Sir. Can you tell me your name please? Yes, it's Green, Thomas Green.

Librarian: Green, OK. I'm afraid I can't find your name on the computer. Are you a member of the library?

Customer: I used to be, but my membership expired last year, and I've been too busy to come in and renew it.

Librarian: Then you need to take out another membership before you can reserve a book.

Customer: Can I do that now?

Librarian: Yes, no problem. I just need to take down some details. First of all, I need your address.

Customer: Sure, it's 21 Southern Avenue.

Librarian: And your telephone number?

Customer: Home is 6 double 6,7,4,6,9,4. And work is double 7,4,3,8,6,3,4.

Librarian: And your postcode?

Customer: SA286.

Librarian: That's fine then. You can collect your membership card anytime after next week. Now you say you'd like to reserve a book, is that right?

Customer: Yes, that's correct. It's called *Western Minds*.

Librarian: *Western Minds*. And what category would that come under?

Customer: Actually I'm not quite sure. I don't think sociology, although it could be. And it's almost certainly not anthropology. I would say psychology.

Librarian: OK, let me just see now. Ah, yes, here it is. I will put a reservation on that for you.

Customer: That's great. When will I be able to collect it?

Librarian: You must collect it sometime within next week. If you leave it longer than five days I will have to take the reservation off.

Customer: OK, well, I'm working tomorrow and Wednesday. Thursday morning would be OK, or Friday afternoon.

Librarian: The library closes early on Fridays so it'll have to be the day before.

Customer: OK, no problem. I'll call in just before lunch. Say about 11:30, would that be OK?

Librarian: 11:30 would be fine.

第三周　星期三　旅行

场景一：与朋友谈论度假计划

You are now going to listen to two friends, Brain and Bob, discussing their holiday plans.

First, you have some time to look at questions 1-8.

30 second pause

Listen to the conversation and answer questions 1-8.

Brain: Hi, Bob. Did you enjoy Tim's party the other night?

Bob: Yes, I did. It was really nice to see everyone again after all these years.

Brain: I know what you mean. Anyway, what about that holiday we were talking about? Do you still want to go ahead with it?

Bob: You bet I do! I've been very busy at work and I really need a break. You Know, just lie in the sun and relax. Maybe read a book or two.

Brain: Really? I was thinking about something more active. You know, maybe do some sightseeing or swimming. Maybe even some surfing if you're up to it.

Bob: I think I could be persuaded. Yes, why not? Surfing sounds like fun to me. But where had you got in mind? The destination, I mean.

Brain: Well, I called into the travel agent this morning and picked up some brochures. Here, take a look. But do you prefer to go abroad, or just somewhere in UK?

Bob: I don't think I can afford the time to go abroad, maybe just somewhere out of England.

Brain: Ok, that's fine with me. look, I've got one on the South of Wales which looks really nice. Or there's Northern Ireland if you fancy some adventure. Or, of course, there's Scotland.

Bob: Scotland. Sounds good. I haven't been there for a long time. Look at that picture. Blue sky, white sounds and …

Brain: I know, but have you seen the price? ￡350 for one week. And that doesn't even include the hotel!

Bob: Yeah, it is a bit expensive, isn't it? What about the South of Wales?

Brain: That's a lot cheaper. In fact, there is a special deal on at the moment. 7 days, including the hotel, for only ￡250.

Bob: Let's have a look at Northern Ireland.

Brain: I already have. It's far too expensive.

Bob: Wales it is then, I guess. But can we choose the hotel? I don't want to get there and find they've put us up in a really cheap place miles away from the beach.

Brain: No problem. There are three hotels to choose from. This one looks the best.

Bob: Which one? Brand View or the Orientals?

Brain: The Brand View. It's only a 10 minute walk from the beach. Half that if you take a bus. And breakfast is included in the price. We do have to pay a surcharge, though.

Bob: How much?

Brain: ￡10. But I guess it's worth it. The location is great and they even have an outdoor swimming pool if you don't want to leave the hotel.

Bob: What about a gym?

Brain: Oh yes, they have a gymnasium that the guests can use. There's no tennis court, though I'm afraid, or massage service, which I know you like. There is a sauna.

Bob: That's OK. I can live without a massage service, which I know you like. Sounds great.

Brain: Great. And the price is certainly too good to miss.

场景二：导游介绍伦敦塔轶事

You are going to hear someone talking about The Tower of London.

First you have some time to look at the questions1-6.

30 second pause

Now listen to the conversation and answer the questions.

I'm Helen. Today, we're taking you on a journey of discovery inside one of the darkest places in London, The Tower of London. I have quite a few stories for you about this dark place.

The Tower of London was built 900 years ago by the king of England at the time-William the

Conqueror. The Tower is famous for its role as a prison and a place of execution.

As I said it's a dark place, I will show you some stories to you, you would know how dark the place was.

As a place of execution, people, in ancient times, were mainly beheaded with one stroke of the axe. What happened next was standard: the head was impaled on a soldier's pike—a spear-like weapon—and it was carried through the streets of London and left on London Bridge as a warning to other would-be traitors. But it also served as an early form of birdfeeder.

Here is another dark story. Around 400 years ago…King Edward IV died and left his brother Richard, Duke of Gloucester, to look after his young sons, one of whom was the new king.

But Uncle Richard locked up his nephews into the Tower of London and seized the throne for himself. The poor boys were only 14 and 10 years old. And then one day the boys simply disappeared within the tower.

Their disappearance was a mystery for nearly 200 years. In 1674, workmen on the south side of the White Tower, removing an old stairwell, found a box. Inside were the remains of two small boys. Experts at the time claimed these to be the bones of the princes.

And on orders of King Charles II, they were placed in Westminster Abbey, in Innocents' Corner, which is named in their honour.

Well, you may think the Tower of London couldn't get any scarier, here is another surprise.

Guy Fawkes, you may have heard the name before, but do you know what he did? Well, to make it simple, he tried to blow up the parliament in 1605, but he failed. He was bound by his wrists and ankles to two spindles. These were then set in the rack. By means of a ratchet mechanism, the spindles turned in opposite directions. So he began to stretch.

On the rack you can stretch a man nearly six inches and then things go rather badly wrong. Joints get pulled apart and your joints are held together with ligament and tendon. You might have known that. But it will be news to some of you that ligament and tendon are stronger than bone.

No one can survive the torturous rack. Not even Guy Fawkes.

There are loads of stories like these, but they are just stories. I hope these would not stop you from visiting it.

场景三：旅游公司合作

You are now going to hear two travel agents talking on the phone about a bridge climbing in UK. First you have some time to look at questions1-5.

45 second pause

Now listen to the conversation and answer the questions.

Jack: Hello. World Bridge Climb Club.

Lucy: Oh, hi! It's Lucy calling from Global Touring in Beijing, China. Good afternoon.

Jack: Well, it's good morning, in fact.

Lucy: Oh, of course. We're eight hours ahead of you, aren't we? So what's the time over there in London?

Jack: It's nine in the morning… and how can I help you?

Lucy: Well, I've got some clients who would like to climb the Bridge you advertised online when they come to London. Is that possible?

Jack: Absolutely!

Lucy: It sounds like a fantastic thing to do. But I do have a couple of questions before I go ahead with any bookings.

Jack: Sure.

Lucy: First of all. Are there any restrictions on the number of people who can climb at the same time? I only ask because we've got a group of 24 people who want to do this together.

Jack: Well, there's actually a limit of 12 people for every climb. So we'd have to split them up, I'm afraid.

Lucy: OK. That sounds fine. And what's the cost? I had a look at your website, but I just want to confirm the prices.

Jack: Well, there are a couple of different rates depending on when you want to go. During the week, it's 89 pounds , and it costs 99 at the weekends.

Lucy: So, 89 weekdays …

Jack: That's for an adult, and for a child it's 49 pounds during the week.

Lucy: And how long does it take?

Jack: It takes about two hours.

Lucy: Wow! So will they be climbing for all that time?

Jack: No, no. they need one more hour involving comprehensive safety briefing and demonstration on the ground.

Lucy: Ah ha!

Jack: And after getting to the top of the bridge they need one more hours to come back down.

Lucy: Right, that's four hours together. And if you don't mind my asking, is it safe? Have you had anybody fall off?

Jack: Well, safety is our top priority. Everyone wears a safety harness while they're climbing. It's quite secure.

Lucy: Oh, good! And the view must be fantastic from up there. Great for taking photos.

Jack: Yes, the view is fantastic, but you're not actually permitted to carry cameras with you, I'm afraid.

Lucy: Oh! That's a shame. Why's that?

Jack: Because there's a risk of dropping them down onto the cars below, and that could be very dangerous.

Lucy: So does that mean we don't have any photographic record of the climb?

Jack: Do not worry. We have our own photographer who goes with you and takes lots of shots for you.

Lucy: That's great. I will only have to reconfirm with my clients and call you back soon.

Jack: Great, good bye.

Lucy: bye.

第三周 星期四 健康和医疗

场景一：牙齿健康调查

You are going to hear a conversation between two people talking about taking care of teeth. First you have some time to look at the questions1-7.

30 second pause

Now listen to the conversation and answer the questions.

(I=Interviewer R=Respondent)

I: Excuse me, I am conducting a survey about how people take care of their teeth. Do you mind answering a few questions?

R: I have some minutes, OK, go ahead.

I: Thank you. Let me just go directly to the topic. First of all, how often do you clean your teeth?

R: About 3 or sometimes more times a day.

I: At what time of day do you clean your teeth?

R: I try to brush after every meal and before bed. Sometimes I brush before my work. I do not like smelling other people's bad breath and I am sure they don't want to be near mine.

I: You are very considerate. Next, you know, nowadays there are more things available in chemist shops to help with dental hygiene. Do you use anything other than an ordinary toothbrush and toothpaste for dental hygiene purposes?

R: Well, I actually use a herbal toothpaste that has no fluoride. It is actually a bit cheaper and has a very nice minty smell. There is nothing special about my toothbrush.

I: Next, it's about gums, you chew gums right?

R: Yes, I do, a lot actually.

I: Has a dentist or any of the dental staff given you advice on caring for your gums?

R: Not really.

I: Some people go to a dentist near to their work. Do you usually take time off work when you go to the dentist?

R: No. Only if I cannot get an appointment in my own time.

I: How much work time does a dental visit usually take?

R: About an hour, usually.

I: Would you say that nowadays you go to the dentist more often, about the same or less often than you did 5 years ago?

R: About as often. That is to say, as rarely as I can manage to make it.

I: What is your attitude to dentists?

R: Well, I think it is awkward, uncomfortable and stressful to have work done on your teeth. I do not like having my teeth drilled. I don't much care for the needles and I really dislike having my teeth pulled out. I have to force myself to relax. I just find it a bit stressful. The other factor is the expense. Dental work is not especially cheap and I don't carry dental insurance. So I have to bear the entire cost. I guess that's pretty much I can tell, and I am afraid I have to go now.

I: Thank you so much for your time. Have a nice day.

R: Thank you. Good bye.

场景二：节食

You are going to hear someone talking about being on a diet.

First you have some time to look at the questions1-8.

30 second pause

Now listen to the conversation and answer the questions.

Good evening, ladies and gentlemen. I am very honored to have this opportunity to share with you about a thing or two on dieting.

As everybody knows, dieting generally means to eat less to lose weight, although some people diet for medical or ethical reasons. Today I'd like to talk to you dieting to stay healthy.

The right dieting concept should be, I am afraid, keeping a nutrition balance. Do not overeat, but still have enough energy for all activities.

First of all, it is very necessary to dispense with large meals and fast food. Fast foods are convenient, but they have little nutritional value. They are full of fats that are very unhealthy but contain little in the way of proteins and minerals that your body needs. So avoid them!

Rice and pasta is cheap. It is also very healthy because it is high in essential carbohydrates which are essential for providing you with energy. But don't eat too much because carbohydrates are stored by the body in the form of fat. Fruit is another very good source of vitamins and minerals. And you can eat as much fruit or vegetables as you wish.

Meat is an excellent source of protein, which is essential for a healthy body. But too much meat is bad for you, especially red meat such as lamb, beef and pork. So don't eat too much. White meat, such as chicken, however, is much healthier. And it's a lot cheaper than red meat, so you can eat more of it.

Fish, however, is a healthy alternative to meat. Steamed or boiled fish is good for you. And you can eat as much fish as you like without any danger of putting on weight. The same goes for vegetables that are full of vitamins and minerals and essential for maintaining a healthy lifestyle. But don't overcook them, because it might lose much of the natural goodness.

You can eat as much bread as you wish. It is an excellent health food. But avoid white bread. Instead eat whole wheat or brown bread.

But one of the main ways of eating healthily is to avoid big meals. Try to eat three medium size meals a day. And if you do feel the need to eat something between meals then fruit or yoghurt is an excellent substitute. But avoid sweets and chocolate.

Well, that's all from me today, but I have put together this handbook on healthy eating which contains a lot of information on which type of food to eat, and which ones you should avoid as well as some very handy recipes.

场景三：中西医

You are going to hear three students, Annice, Carl and Joy, discussing about Chinese medicine and Western medicine.

First, you have some time to look at questions 1-6.

30 second pause

Now listen to the conversation and answer the questions.

Annice: Hi Joy, how's it going? I hear you've started your new course, on … what is it? Holistic medicine?

Joy: Hello, Annice. Yes, that's right … well, kind of. I'm going to specialize in acupuncture actually.

Carl: Mmm … I've never been sure exactly what holistic medicine involves. Can you explain?

Joy: OK. Basically, holistic is about the "whole" or entire system or person. Traditionally, the Chinese regarded a person as an integrated body, mind and spirit. So holistic medicine takes the whole physical, mental and emotional entity of a person into account. It places more emphasis on overall health and well being.

Carl: I thought western medicine did that too.

Joy: Not really. Conventional western medicine is symptomatic; it tends to diagnose and treat specific symptoms, or refer patients to specialists who are expert in one field, say cardiology or urology, who can treat a heart or kidney problem very effectively, but who don't necessarily relate their diagnosis and treatment to the whole person or to their lifestyle habits.

Annice: Well, so what? A sick person just wants to feel better, doesn't he? If I go to the doctor with a pain, I want it alleviated and cleared up quickly.

Carl: Ahh, I think I understand: maybe a doctor prescribes painkillers, but the root cause of the pain may still be there, isn't that right, Joy?

Joy: Yes, exactly. Holistic medicine aims to prevent the causes; it's preventive rather than reactive.

Annice: OK, I think I understand that, but tell us some more about acupuncture. I've seen it done and I can't believe that the person can't feel those great big needles sticking out of them! And some people get it done even when they're not ill, isn't that right?

Joy: Well, yes, because of the difference in attitudes. Acupuncture is holistic in that it works on the whole body's energy system. Chinese traditional doctors believe that symptoms and illnesses reflect a blockage or imbalance in the energy channels and that if these are cleared or rebalanced, the arthritis, skin complaint or whatever the patient is suffering from will disappear.

Annice: But does it actually work?

Joy: Of course! Our instructor has told us many success stories where people who have been suffering for years have completely recovered from all kinds of illnesses: migraine, arthritis, drug addiction, high blood pressure, bronchitis, you name it.

Annice: And what does the doctor do when you first visit? Stick you full of needles on the spot?

Joy: No, but I am in a hurry now. Why don't you guys come to my room this afternoon? I would like to show you something, so that you may be more convinced, right?

Annice: That's great. I would love to know more about the magic thing, so see you then.

Carl: See you.

第三周　星期五　生活

场景一：讨论生日聚会

You are going to listen to two people, Sue and Sarah, discussing a birthday party.

First you have some time to look at questions 1-7.

30 second pause

Now listen to the conversation and answer the questions.

Sarah: Hi, Sue.

Sue: Hi, Sarah. I remember that next Tuesday is your birthday, right?

Sarah: No, it's Shirley's birthday Tuesday. Mine's the day after.

Sue: Oh, how are you going to celebrate it this time?

Sarah: Actually, I was thinking of having a joint birthday party.

Sue: That sounds great.

Sarah: Yes, but can you please help me to brainstorm some ideas about how to prepare for it?

Sue: Sure, that's my favorite part. Firstly, where were you thinking of holding it?

Sarah: I think my place, it's rather small though. It'll be too expensive to hire a room, and Sue's room is smaller than mine.

Sue: So what type of food were you thinking about? You won't cook that day, will you?

Sarah: No, I'd order some food and get them delivered.

Sue: Wow, that's a good idea. What type of food, then? Italian, Japanese, Thai maybe?

Sarah: Not everyone likes Japanese or Thai. So I thought we could order pizza.

Sue: OK, well, there's an Italian restaurant near my home. We could buy it from there. It'll be cheaper than having it delivered.

Sarah: Why not? Would you mind arranging that, and I'll sort out the music. What do you think, dance music, classical or jazz?

Sue: Dance music is too loud. And I think classical is too much. I'd go for some jazz, if I were you.

Sarah: OK then, Jazz it is.

Sue: Don't forget the drinks.

Sarah: Oh, yes. I knew there was something. Beer, wine? Or what about spirits?

Sue: I wouldn't buy any spirits. Beer and wine is the best option.

Sarah: What type of wine? White or red?

Sue: I'd get both, that way you can satisfy all tastes.

Sarah: Right then. I can buy that from the local supermarket. Is there anything I've forgotten?

Sue: What about the time?

Sarah: Do you think 7:00 is a good time?

Sue: Most people finish work around 6.00 o' clock. You'd better prolong it a little bit.

Sarah: OK then, 7:30 it is. So I'll see you then.

场景二：有机牛排

Listen to two work colleagues discussing the pros and cons of choosing organic food.

First you have some time to look at questions 1-5.

30 second pause

Now listen to the conversation and answer the questions.

Victor: What's that you're eating, Johnson, not a piece of steak, is it? I thought you were vegetarian!

Johnson: It is steak. I was never vegetarian. But it's organic. I just like eating natural food.

Victor: How can meat be organic?

Johnson: It means the animal isn't full of strange hormones, or has never ate cereal that's been genetically modified or sprayed with pesticides. That sort of thing.

Victor: But can you taste the difference?

Johnson: Sure, and at least I know I am eating something natural. I don't want to get terrible diseases.

Victor: Yes, but there's no proof that terrible diseases are related to non-organic food.

Johnson: I just don't want to take the risk. It takes a long time to know, and many scientists are doing research on them.

Victor: There are stories saying that some companies are putting small quantities of chemicals into food, and track the reactions secretly.

Johnson: Really, that is terrible. I think the government should ban that.

Victor: Yes, and if the newspapers found a company was deliberately selling an unsafe product, their share price would crash and they'd be out of business in no time.

Johnson: They may go out of business soon if they don't start selling organic food themselves. Have you seen what's in the supermarkets these days? They say sales of organic food have risen by 35%.

Victor: It's still more expensive. You've got to compare the price, which is at least double, with the risk you're running, which is absolutely minimal if you ask me. And how many people farm organically in this country, anyway? It's not even 1%.

Johnson: Well, it's more like 20% in other parts of Europe. And the more people buy it, the more the price will come down. It's better for the environment, anyway. We can't keep playing around with our food without consequences, you know. Look at all the animal diseases we've had recently.

Victor: True, there are always stories in the papers of salmonella in eggs, sheep suffering from foot and mouth disease, cows with…

Johnson: Well, we'd better stop there. I want to finish my lunch now!

场景三：看朋友的孩子

You are going to hear a conversation between husband and wife about their friend's baby. First you have some time to look at the questions1-7.

30 second pause

Now listen to the conversation and answer the questions.

Wife: Hi, darling. I've just had some good news. Susan has had her baby.

Husband: Oh, that is good news; do you know when she had it?

Wife: The tenth of August.

Husband: Oh, my father was born on August the tenth.

Wife: Yes, I have realized that.

Husband: Well, was it a boy or a girl?

Wife: It's a boy.

Husband: And what are they going to call him?

Wife: Tom. Tom Whitehead. It sounds quite good, don't you think?

Husband: Yes, that is an interesting name.

Wife: You know he's quite a big baby. He weighed four and a quarter kilos.

Husband: That does sound big, four and a quarter kilos.

Wife: And he's forty-six centimeters.

Husband: That's a long boy. Tall parents. He'll grow up to be over two metres, I'd say.

Wife: With masses of curly black hair. You know, it is so beautiful. I think we should go together to visit them in hospital.

Husband: Yes, what time is good?

Wife: What about tomorrow afternoon at around l p m?

Husband: That's OK with me. What's the address again?

Wife: It's 25 Bluefield Road.

Husband: I know that place, we can drive there tomorrow.

Wife: That's great, I am so exciting about it. Now what should we take? We must take them something.

Husband: I always think flowers are good to take to someone in hospital, don't you?

Wife: Well, not really. Flowers might not be good to the baby. I think it's much better to take something for the baby.

Husband: OK, then you make the decision. I am not good at that.

Wife: Yes, I will go to the supermarket tomorrow morning, and I will see what we can buy there.

Husband: Great, I will come back home to pick you up after I finish my work, OK?

Wife: Yes, maybe you can pick me up at the supermarket. We can go from the market, it's much closer.

Husband: Great, I think I should start preparing for my presentation now.

Wife: Yes, I will go to watch a movie on the TV.

第三周 星期六 环保

场景一：回收电池

You are going to hear someone talking about battery recycling.

First you have some time to look at the questions1-5.

30 second pause

Now listen to the conversation and answer the questions.

We use batteries to power any number of household items: remote controls, cameras, flashlights and portable power tools among others. According to the U. S. Environmental Protection Agency, each year Americans buy almost 3 billion dry-cell batteries to power these common household items. The average American discards eight batteries each year.

And as we do with other items that we no longer need, it's tempting to just throw used batteries in the trash, but that would be a mistake.

Inside a battery, heavy metals react with chemical electrolyte to generate power. The metals found in batteries include mercury, lead, cadmium and nickel.

If batteries are not recycled, these metals can pollute the environment.

Depending on how batteries are discarded, the metals can be released into the air or remain behind in the ash created by incineration.

Batteries that are disposed of in landfills can leach into the soil, contaminating groundwater supplies. This is especially true of automotive batteries, which contain lead and acid.

Instead consumers are encouraged to separate batteries from the regular household trash and find a proper place to dispose of the batteries.

Rechargeable batteries have reduced the amount of batteries that need to be recycled. But even so, the majority of batteries are single-use.

Batteries can be divided into two broad categories: dry-cell and wet-cell batteries.

The dry-cell type is used in most consumer electronics, and includes alkaline and carbon zinc batteries and lithium batteries .

Wet-cell batteries are typically found in cars, boats and motorcycles.

Both types of batteries can be recycled.

场景二：保护宠物免受野生动物攻击

You are going to hear someone talking about protecting pets from being attacked by wild animals.

First you have some time to look at the questions1-6.

30 second pause

Now listen to the conversation and answer the questions.

Protecting Your Pet from Coyotes

Coyotes look like small wolves, resembling dogs. They view your pets as food and especially pounce on small animals and cats. What's more, they even attack and kill larger dogs. Although nocturnal creatures, they can look for pets during the day and then return at night for their prey. Creatures of habit, they're found at the same spots with habitual routes at night.

A few preventative measures include…

Install a wooden fence—Although they've been known to climb over high fences, you're better off with a wooden fence at least 5.5 feet tall. Wooden fences are better than chain length ones because it's harder to climb over them. Also, safeguard your pets from a coyote digging under the fence by burying large rocks outside the fence line.

Supervise your pet outdoors—Never leave your pets alone when outdoors. By supervising them, you can reduce the odds of an attack. Walk your dog for nightly potty breaks before dark, as nighttime is the most likely time for coyotes to be on the prowl. Make your cats outside pets if you live in an area susceptible to wildlife, such as woods.

Make noise on walks—By making loud noises outside, you'll discourage a coyote from coming close. It's also best to have others join you when walking your dog.

Never leave food or garbage outside—Make sure your garbage cans are stored safely in your garage and bring in all pet food and water dishes. Get rid of any birdseed houses as this can also invite unwanted wildlife to your yard.

Neuter your dog—Because they belong to the canine family, coyotes can mate with unaltered domestic dogs. The scent of an unsprayed female dog in heat can easily lure a male coyote. On the other hand, male dogs can be attracted to female coyotes. Therefore, dog owners should spray or neuter their pets to prevent a possible tragedy, especially if they live in wooded areas.

Pick fruit off trees—It's better if you don't have fruit trees if you have pets. However, if you do, be sure and pick the fruit so as not to entice coyotes to your property.

场景三：温室效应

You are now going to hear someone talking about greenhouse effect.

First you have some time to look at the questions1-7.

30 second pause

Now listen to the conversation and answer the questions.

Greenhouse gasses have no harmful effects. They are, in fact, the reason that this planet is warm enough for us to survive. Without the greenhouse effect, much of the sunlight that reaches the surface would reflect or be re-radiated right back into space, and the surface temperatures would be about 33℃ colder than it is. Life could not exist in that environment.

There is some concern that "too much" greenhouse gasses in the atmosphere will cause an "enhanced greenhouse effect", also known as "global warming". But the greenhouse gasses have a built-in mechanism that mitigates this. Greenhouse gasses can only absorb infrared radiation within narrow bands of wavelengths. Each greenhouse gas has a profile of these "absorption spectra", but a given greenhouse gas cannot absorb any radiation outside of its own spectrum.

When the concentration of a given greenhouse gas, let's say Carbon Dioxide, is low, its spectrum is not a limit on how much radiation it can absorb, because there is plenty of radiation in its spectrum, and each additional unit of CO_2 absorbs its full potential of infrared. But, as the concentration of CO_2 increases, there is less and less infrared radiation in its spectrum to absorb, and each additional unit of CO_2 therefore absorbs less radiation. At some point, all of the infrared radiation in CO_2's absorption spectrum is absorbed, and that point, additional CO_2 in the atmosphere will not absorb any more infrared radiation. This is referred to as "saturation" of the wavelengths.

In some cases, the absorption spectra of two different greenhouse gasses overlap. For example, Carbon Dioxide and Water Vapor. At the wavelengths where CO_2's and H_2O's absorption spectrum overlap, they are both absorbing infrared radiation at those wavelengths. This means that each molecule of CO_2, in addition to competing with other molecules of CO_2, is also competing with H_2O to absorb the available radiation. So, along those wavelengths, the "wavelength competition effect" further limits the amount of radiation CO_2 can absorb.

One more thing on this subject. We humans have no control over the concentration of water vapor in the atmosphere, and it varies drastically, both temporally and geographically. Nevertheless, even at its lowest concentration, Water Vapor is far and away the largest contributor to the overall greenhouse effect. Molecule for molecule, it's not as powerful a greenhouse gas as CO_2, but there's just so much more Water Vapor that its overall effect dwarfs that of all other greenhouse gasses. If there were no carbon dioxide in the atmosphere, the greenhouse effect would vary drastically, right along with the concentration of Water Vapor in the atmosphere. The presence of CO_2, obviously, helps to "pick up the slack" when and where water vapor concentration is low. But, when you consider the overlap between the absorption spectra, what you have is built-in thermostat. When water vapor concentration is low, CO_2 absorbs more of the radiation that water vapor would be absorbing, if it were there, thus keeping the temperature somewhat warmer when the lack of water vapor would tend to make it colder. But, where and when water vapor concentration is high, as discussed in the previous paragraph, it has to compete, along some part of its absorption spectrum, with CO_2 to absorb infrared radiation, and thus the absorption by both is limited. So, a high concentration of CO_2 in the atmosphere is a good thing, as it helps to mitigate large swings in temperature that would be caused by the highly variable concentration of water vapor.

第三周　星期日　科研

场景一：讨论科研

You are going to hear a conversation between Joice and Kyle about essay writing.

First you have some time to look at the questions1-6.

30 second pause

Now listen to the conversation and answer the questions.

Joice: Hi, Kyle, have you thought about the essay we have to write… the one how students learn through the media… how shall we write it?

Kyle: Well, I've thought about it yesterday and I think we should divide the essay into two parts. First of all, we'd have to look at some examples of each type of media…

Joice: Yes, what they are… then we could describe how we can use each medium so that students can learn something from each one.

Kyle: Exactly. Maybe we could draw up a table and look at examples of each medium in turn. Let's see, the different forms of media would be… the print media…

Joice: Yes. We have things like books and magazine, that sort of thing…

Kyle: Um, and things like maps…

Joice: Yes. And then there are the audio forms of media…where students can listen. CDs and radios etc.

Kyle: And the audio-visual media, which can be seen as well as heard…film, television…and videos.

Joice: Yes, but there are computers as well, we may call them electronic media. Almost all the families have computers now.

Kyle: Yes, I believe it. Well that's a good list to start with…we're really getting somewhere. so let's move on to when each type of medium could be used. I think we could start by trying to identify the best situation for each type of media.

Joice: What do you mean?

Kyle: I'm talking about whether each medium should be used with different sized groups, For example, we could look at pictures, and ask whether they're more useful for an individual student, a few students together or a full class in this case, I'd say pictures are best examples with individual student, because they give them an opportunity to let their imaginations run wild.

Joice: Yes, I see…

Kyle: Let's take tapes next. they're best suited to small group of students, This way, students don't feel isolated, because they can get help from their friends. Computers are the same…I think they're better with small numbers of students and they're hardly ever useful with a whole class. Videos, however, are ideal for use with everyone present in the class.

Joice: And what about books, what would you recommend for them? Books are ideal for students to use by themselves.

Kyle: I agree…

场景二：论文写作

You are now going to listen to a professor talking about how to write an introduction.

First you have some time to look at the questions1-12.

45 second pause

Now, listen to the introduction and fill in the blanks of the summary.

Whatever you are writing—an essay, a report, an article, a thesis, a journal, a literature review, or any other piece of academic writing—the introduction will be the first thing the reader sees. If an introduction is poorly written or constructed, if it is boring, if it does not tell readers what they need to know, if it does not help readers to orient themselves to your paper—then you have lost your readers' goodwill right from the beginning, and can be sure of losing marks, no matter how well the rest of the assignment is constructed.

It's essential, then, that you get the introduction right. This means that you must know what the introduction is supposed to do, what sorts of things must go into the introduction, how to write and structure the introduction properly, and how to interest your reader from the start.

An introduction should do the following:

- alert a reader's interest
- indicate the scope and direction of the paper, and act as a navigation guide to its reading.
- show the reader how you are interpreting and approaching the question
- provide a context for the main issue
- indicate the focus of the paper
- indicate your conclusion and point of view

Below is an introduction which would be suitable for a 1500-2000 word essay on intercultural communication. This introduction will be analysed to show its content and structure.

The question is that workplace diversity is now recognised as an important feature in organisations, especially in multicultural nations like Australia. What communication problems might arise in a culturally diverse workplace, and how can managers best deal with them?

The introduction may go like this:

Over the past twenty-five years, since Australia embraced multiculturalism as a policy, issues of intercultural communication have become more and more prominent in the workplace. However, until relatively recently, little had been written on these issues, and even now, many organisational managers have no training or knowledge of how to deal with communication problems, even though most workplaces are staffed by people of diverse cultures. Particular problem areas include the difficulties that some non-English speakers have in understanding safety instructions (figures produced by the ABS in 1997 show that migrant workers have a higher incidence of accidents at the workplace); an ignorance of the different forms of non-verbal communication used by other cultures (for example, it is considered impolite in some societies for an employee to look directly at his or her employer), which can lead to misunderstandings and unpleasantness; and the lack of knowledge about differing expectations. Based on interviews with managers and staff in six organisations (public and commercial), this report examines these three problem areas, and shows that many of the difficulties faced by both natives and migrants in the workforce are caused by a lack of awareness of, and training in, intercultural communication.

场景三：申请项目基金

You are going to hear someone talking about applying for fund for a project.

First you have some time to look at the questions1-7.

30 second pause

Now listen to the conversation and answer the questions.

Good morning, ladies and gentlemen. I am speaking today on behalf of my research team, which consists of two other primary teachers and a doctorial student in addition to myself.

Actually, all of us are teachers with at least five years of experience in teaching children reading. We have applied for this grant because we are extremely interested in investigating problems with reading habits amongst people in the primary level. Our specific research questions are, firstly, "does having bedroom TV lower a child's reading age"? And secondly, is there any relationship between good reader and having good parental teaching?

Now if I can just give you a little background on our proposal.

Our motivation to investigate this came out of a short survey on some 8 years old children. There are about 14 very poor readers in our school. They were watching TV for more than 5 hours daily. There are another 10 average readers who only watch TV for about 2 hours a day, which obviously indicate that they have more time learning reading with mum and dad. Now what we like to do with our research is to get more information from more pupils, parents and teachers.

We plan to survey 150 children, so we need some money to cover the materials and gifts that we give to the children. We also need to consider the expenses involved in visiting schools, since we have to visit at least 8 schools if we want to have that many pupils. By careful budgeting, we think we need 1800 pounds for that. And our second plan is to interview 50 parents, which need another 1500 pounds, apart from that, we have to consider the cost used for statistic analysis as well as the additional fee for the computer center, which in total is about 1000 pounds. Therefore the grant we want to apply for is about 3,300 in total.

It sounds a little bit high, but I have to remind you of the tremendous value of our research.

We feel strongly that our research will bring great benefits to many different groups. We hope it would help parents in their struggles to improve their children's academic standards, and most importantly to help the kids with learning problems by changing their habits and life styles. Finally, we think the teachers will benefit as well, because the difference among pupils in the same class would not be that impossibly big any more.

Any way, we think this research is very valuable. We really hope you can help us to make this study possible. Thank you very much.

第四周　七天模拟，强力冲刺

第四周　星期一　Model Test 1

IELTS PRACTICE TEST

LISTENING

NARRATOR

You will hear a number of different recordings and you will have to answer questions on what you hear. There will be time for you to read the instructions and questions, and you will have a chance to check your work.

All the recordings will be played ONCE only. The test is in four sections. At the end of the real test you will be given ten minutes to transfer your answers to an answer sheet.

Now turn to Section 1.

SECTION 1

You will hear an interview conversation. First you have some time to look at questions 1-6.

15 second pause

You will see that there is an example that has been done for you. On this occasion only, the conversation relating to this will be played first.

Interviewee: Good afternoon, I called this morning, and I come for an interview…

Interviewer: Ah, you must be Miss Smith?

Interviewee: Yes, Green Smith.

Interviewer: Take a seat please.

Interviewee: Thank you.

Interviewer: Ok, would you mind answering a few questions?

Interviewee: No, not at all.

Interviewer: Ok, first of all, where do you live?

Interviewee: My address is 32 Acacia Avenue.

Interviewer: And your post code?

Narrator: *The interviewee said "my address is 32 Acacia Avenue", so the correct answer is Acacia Avenue.*

Now We shall begin.

You should answer the questions as you listen because you will not hear the recording a second time.

Now listen carefully and answer questions 1-6.

Interviewee: Good afternoon, I called this morning, and I come for an interview…

Interviewer: Ah, you must be Miss Smith?

Interviewee: Yes, Green Smith.

Interviewer: Take a seat please.

Interviewee: Thank you.

Interviewer: Ok, would you mind answering a few questions?

Interviewee: No, not at all.

Interviewer: Ok, first of all, where do you live?

Interviewee: My address is 32 Acacia Avenue.

Interviewer: And your post code?

Interviewee: It's RA67BU.

Interviewer: I see, you said you are a student, right?

Interviewee: Yes, I am a junior student in University.

Interviewer: What do you study then?

Interviewee: My major is photography.

Interviewer: Did you get some working experiences?

Interviewee: Yes, actually I have taken three part time jobs before.

Interviewer: May I know what they are?

Interviewee: Sure, the first job I did is working as an assistant in a flower shop.

Interviewer: How long have you worked there?

Interviewee: I have worked there for about three months. I quite liked that job, but they moved to a new place, which is too far away from my university.

Interviewer: I see, you said, three part-time jobs. What was the second one?

Interviewee: I later worked in a nursery to take care of some elder people.

Interviewer: Oh, really, how do you like that?

Interviewee: Well, it is not bad, being with elder people. I feel I am very needed, and I was very proud of myself because, frankly speaking, it is not easy to do that job.

Interviewer: I understand.

Interviewee: But it took too much of my time, so I had to quit, you know, I have to study at the same time.

Interviewer: Yes, of course.

Interviewee: So I went to a restaurant, and have been working there as a waitress till last week.

Before you hear the rest of the conversation, you have some time to look at questions 7-10.

15 second pause

Now listen and answer questions 7-10.

Interviewer: Why is that then?

Interviewee: Well, you know. I realized that I need to start using what I am learning in the university, so that I can get some experience.

Interviewer: I see. OK, do you have something to ask?

Interviewee: Well, yes, what do I have to do in this job?

Interviewer: Well, since we have three photographers, generally it is good enough, but only recently, we became very busy, so we need somebody to work as a part-timer, so that they can get some break.

Interviewee: I see, that's no problem.

Interviewer: OK, the last question, what time do you prefer to work, weekends, evening, holidays or lunch time?

Interviewee: OK, I have no problems with weekends and holidays, but I am not very sure about evenings, because sometimes I have to take some evening courses, not many though. And I can not make it at lunch time, because it takes a long to commute here.

Interviewer: I see, that would be fine, if you work at weekends and holidays, it will be good, but maybe sometimes you will have to come in the evening, we will discuss with you in advance of course.

Interviewee: Great, thank you.

Interviewer: Ok, when can you start working then?

Interviewee: Anytime starting from now.

Interviewer: That's wonderful, I will call you when necessary, what is your phone number again?

Interviewee: It's 3598330.

Interviewer: OK, welcome aboard.

Interviewee: Thank you very much.

Interviewer: Good bye.

Interviewee: Good bye.

That's the end of Section One.

You now have half a minute to check your answers.

30 second pause

Now turn to Section Two.

SECTION 2

You are going to listen to two people talking about studying in Australia. First you have some time to look at questions 11-15.

15 second pause

Now listen to the conversation and answer questions 11-15.

Presenter: Welcome here, everyone. first of all, I'd like to introduce today's guest, Professor Speary, who is going to talk to us about studying in Australia. Professor Speary, over to you.

Speaker: Thank you. And welcome, everybody. As introduced, I am going to talk with you about studying in Australia. Only recently, Australia has become a popular place for people to go for further education. As a matter of fact, in order to attract more people to come, the government has been trying its best to provide overseas students a better environment to study. In the following, I will give you some examples.

First of all, the government has made its education system very flexible, so anyone who study here can move through flexible study pathways to gain the right balance of practical skills and theoretical knowledge for your future career.

Australian education providers have worked together to create a well-established system that helps you move easily from one level of study to the next. The Australian Qualifications Framework (AQF) is a national system. Unlike in many other countries, the government carefully oversees quality standards, so you can be confident that you will receive the same high quality education no matter which institution you choose in Australia. The AQF lets you design the study program you require for your individual learning and career options.

The higher education in Australia is especially developed. Australia has 39 universities; 37 of these are government-funded and two are privately-funded.

Now you have some time to look at questions 16-20.

15 second pause

Now listen and answer questions 16-20.

Australian universities offer undergraduate and postgraduate programs. Studying at an Australian university gives students access to a quality education, technologically advanced facilities and expert lecturers. Australian university degrees are widely recognised across the globe, and graduates are highly employable.

And most importantly, Australia is one of the safest countries to stay in. It has a low crime rate, and it is politically stable, and therefore provides a very peaceful society.

Australia is a harmonious nation with equality for all, regardless of gender or race. Australia has never had a civil war, and is free of civil strife. The government is democratically elected, and is not ruled by the military nor based on religion.

The incidence of robbery and assault is relatively low, and Australia has strict anti-gun and drug laws.

Australians trust their police force and their government officials. Bribery and corruption are against the law and are not accepted by society.

Racial discrimination and harassment are also against the law. Overall the Australian people are accepting and welcoming to others.

So international students feel safe, therefore more and more of them would like to come and stay in Australia.

And Australia is a multicultural country, which makes your experience here more rewarding.

Australia accepts people of different nationalities. Its citizens come from nearly 200 countries. Around a quarter of Australia's people were born in another country. Fifteen per cent of Australians speak a language other than English at home.

Whatever your nationality or religion, you'll fit into Australia. There are churches, temples and mosques, cultural support groups, associations, clubs and restaurants by the thousands. You could dine out and enjoy a different cultural cuisine every night.

All in all, Australia is a great place to live-a safe, friendly, multicultural environment which welcomes international students and visitors from around the world.

You can make the most of your study experience by immersing yourself in Australian life. Enjoy the culture, the food, the sights and the people!

That's the end of Section Two.

You now have half a minute to check your answers.

30 second pause

Now turn to Section 3.

SECTION 3

You are going to hear a discussion between a professor and a student about essay writing.

First you have some time to look at questions 21-25.

15 second pause

Now listen to the discussion and answer questions 21-25.

Professor: Come in.

Student: Hello, Professor Smith.

Professor: Ah, hello, George, come and sit down. Now, it's about this essay of yours, am I right?

Student: Yes, the one on language learning strategies.

Professor: Oh, yes, language learning strategies, let's see… what was the exact title again?

Student: How are language learning Strategies…

Professor: Right, here it is: how are language learning strategies acquired.

Student: Yes, that's it.

Professor: Yes, on the whole, I was very pleased with what you wrote, say, you have presented your points of view clearly.

Student: Thank you.

Professor: Did you give the sources for your statistics?

Student: Well, I am not sure, because I got the data on the internet.

Professor: I see, but you still need to put the website on the reference list.

Student: Yes, I will do that.

Professor: Now let's take a look at different parts.

Student: Yes.

Professor: First of all, the introduction, it is a good lead-in, but I think you need explain the background more clearly, to make it more specific, it is in what situation that you want to look at this topic.

Now you have some time to look at questions 26-30.

15 second pause

Now listen to the rest of the discussion and answer questions 26-30.

Student: I see, I think I have put that in the literature review part.

Professor: Well, in your literature review, you tell your readers what has been done in this field, but the background is not necessarily research results.

Student: Ah, I see now. I am always confused about that.

Professor: Now, your literature review. I think you have done a lot of reading, but you cannot just list out the things that you found in the literature, you'd better digest them and put them together so as to make it more enjoyable to read, and more convincing.

Student: I have realized that, but I just feel hard to do that.

Professor: Yes, it is hard; here is what you can do. Put them together randomly, and reorganize them according to different opinions instead of different researchers, maybe you will have a clear view.

Student: That is a good idea. I will do that.

Professor: As for your data, there are adequate information supporting your argument, but I think it would be more straightforward if you use some diagrams to present the figures instead of just listing the statistics there.

Student: I understand, but I think I will have to learn how to make those diagrams.

Professor: Go to talk to Brian. He will give you a lot of help. He is very good at the computer thing, and I have seen his data presentation, very clear, very straightforward.

Student: Thank you, that would be nice. Actually, I was thinking to bump into him this evening, because I need to borrow some books from him.

Professor: That's good. Ok, finally, don't you think you drew a conclusion too abruptly?

Student: Well, I was thinking of putting another transitional paragraph here, but after talking to Tom, he thought that would make the essay too long. So I …

Professor: Well, I insist on your putting in that part, it is longer, but it is clearer and more convincing.

Student: Yes, actually in my last draft, I have that part, so I only need to copy and paste. It's easy now.

Professor: That's great. So, do the changes and you know I am going to Japan for the conference next Friday, I hope to see it before that, is that OK?

Student: Sure, thank you very much for your time.

Professor: You are welcome, good bye.

Student: Good bye.

That's the end of Section Three, you now have half a minute to check your answers.

30 second pause

Now turn to Section 4.

SECTION 4

You are going to listen to someone introducing the history of bicycles. First you have some time to look at questions 31-40.

30 second pause

Now listen carefully and answer questions 31-40.

Vehicles for human transport that have two wheels and require balancing by the rider date back to the early 19th century. The first means of transport making use of two wheels, and thus the archetype of the bicycle, was the German draisine dating back to 1817. The term bicycle was coined in France in the 1860s.

The first mechanically-propelled 2-wheel vehicle was believed to have been built by Kirkpatrick MacMillan, a Scottish blacksmith, in 1839.

The first really popular and commercially successful design was a French one. Initially developed around 1863, it sparked a fashionable craze briefly during 1868-70. Its design was simpler than the Macmillan bicycle; it used rotary cranks and pedals mounted to the front wheel hub.

Since then, bicycles have been developed very quickly. Throughout the history of bikes, people do not only use it for transportation, but also for entertainment, especially as a sport, cycling as we call it today.

Cycling became popular in Europe over the first half of the twentieth century, but it dropped off dramatically in the United States between 1900 and 1910. Automobiles became the preferred means of transportation. Over the 1920s, bicycles gradually became considered children's toys, and by 1940 most bicycles in the United States were made for children. In Europe cycling remained an adult activity, and bicycle racing, commuting, and "cyclotouring" were all popular activities. In addition, specialist bicycles for children appeared before 1916.

Bicycles continued to evolve to suit the varied needs of riders. The derailleur developed in France between 1900 and 1910 among cyclotourists, and was improved over time. Only in the 1930s did European racing organizations allow racers to use gearing; until then they were forced to use a two-speed bicycle. The rear wheel had a cog on either side of the hub. To change gears, the rider had to stop, remove the wheel, flip it around, and remount the wheel. When racers were allowed to use derailleurs, racing times immediately dropped.

At mid-century there were two predominant bicycle styles for recreational cyclists in North America. Heavyweight cruiser bicycles, preferred by the typical cyclist, featuring balloon tires, pedal-driven "coaster" brakes and only one gear, were popular for their durability, comfort, streamlined appearance, and a significant array of accessories, like lights, bells, springer forks, speedometers, etc. Lighter cycles, with hand brakes, narrower tires, and a three-speed hub gearing system, often imported from England, first became popular in the United States in the late 1950s. These comfortable, practical bicycles usually offered generator-powered headlamps, safety reflectors, kickstands, and frame-mounted tire pumps. In the United Kingdom, like the rest of Europe, cycling was seen as less of a hobby, and lightweight but durable bikes had been preferred for decades.

That's the end of Section 4.

You now have half a minute to check your answers.

30 second pause

That's the end of the listening test.

You now have ten minutes to transfer your answers to the listening answer sheet.

第四周　星期二　Model Test2

IELTS PRACTICE TEST

LISTENING

You will hear a number of different recordings and you will have to answer questions on what you hear. There will be time for you to read the instructions and questions, and you will have a chance to check your work.

All the recordings will be played ONCE only. The test is in four sections. At the end of the real test you will be given ten minutes to transfer your answers to an answer sheet.

Now turn to Section 1.

SECTION 1

You will hear a conversation between an IELTS candidate and an IELTS administrator. First you have some time to look at questions 1-5.

15 second pause

Listen to the first part of the conversation and answer questions 1-5.

Candidate: Good afternoon. I'm applying for a Master's programme at a university in the UK. I'm planning to register for the IELTS exam at your centre next month. I have some questions I'd like to ask you before I register, if that's OK.

Administrator: Certainly. Would you be taking the Academic Module or the Training Module?

Candidate: I think it's the Academic one, but I'll have to contact the university just to make sure.

Administrator: You'll probably need the Academic, because most universities don't accept the General Training... And anyway, the procedures to register for the exam are the same for both the General and the Academic modules.

Candidate: Good. My first question is whether I sit all parts of the exam on the same day. I don't live here, you see, and for me it would be more convenient to do all the papers on the same day.

Administrator: Hmm. Unfortunately, the Speaking part often on sundays, and Reading, Writing and Listening tests take place on Saturdays. We can't change the days, I'm afraid.

Candidate: Hmm. That's a pity. Well, never mind. What do I need to bring in order to register?

Administrator: You'll have to fill in the IELTS application form and bring an ID, a copy of your ID and two passport-size photos on a white background.

Candidate: Will any ID do?

Administrator: We only accept original passports and national IDs.

Candidate: That's good to know. Did you say that Reading, Writing and Listening are scheduled for Saturdays?

Administrator: That's right.

Candidate: Will I get a break in between the papers?

Administrator: I'm afraid there aren't any breaks between the papers. It's about three hours straight through the written test. You'll first do Listening, and then Reading followed by the Writing test. This is a standard requirement from Cambridge.

Candidate: OK, and how soon after the test can I pick up my results?

Administrator: It takes two weeks for the results to be processed.

Now look at the questions 6-10.

30 second pause

As the conversation continues, complete questions 6-10.

Candidate: Can you let me know how much it is and the form of payment?

Administrator: The examination fee is HK$ 1,500. You can pay by credit; we also accept cheques. We o nly accept cash as a form of payment in exceptional circumstances.

Candidate: And one last question. Can I mail you the application documents?

Administrator: Certainly. You can send all the documents by registered mail to our address:

13 Supreme Court Road, Hong Kong.

Candidate: You said Supreme Court Road?

Administrator: yes, that's S-U-P-R-E-M-E, C-O-U-R-T.

Candidate: Could I have the zip code as well?

Administrator: Sure, our zip code is SE186.

Candidate: Thanks.

Administrator: You can also e-mail us at ielts. hongkong @ idp. com or phone us at 2827-6362.

Candidate: I think that's all. Thank you very much for the information. Bye.

Administrator: You're welcome. Good-bye.

That's the end of Section One.

You now have half a minute to check your answers.

30 second pause

Now turn to Section Two.

SECTION 2

You are going to listen to someone talking about insomnia.

First you have some time to read questions 11-15.

30 second pause

Now listen to the talk and answer quesitons 11-15.

Good morning, everyone. Today I would like to talk about insomnia. First may I know how many of you have ever had insomnia? Please put up your hands. Thank you, one, two... well, I don't think I will count all of you, but I did not expect so many. But what is insomnia? Generally speaking, anyone who cannot fall into sleep or cannot sleep well, but I have a definition here, which says that insomnia is a symptom that can accompany several sleep, medical and psychiatric disorders, characterized by persistent difficulty falling asleep and/or difficulty staying asleep.

Insomnia can be caused by psychoactive drugs or stimulants, including certain medications, herbs, caffeine, nicotine, cocaine, etc.

According to the United States Department of Health and Human Services in the year 2007, approximately 64 million Americans regularly suffer from insomnia each year.

There are several different degrees of insomnia, three types of insomnia have been clearly identified: transient, acute and chronic.

1. Transient insomnia lasts for less than a week. It can be caused by another disorder, by changes in the sleep environment, by the timing of sleep, severe depression, or by stress. Its consequences-sleepiness and impaired psychomotor performance-are similar to those of sleep deprivation.

2. Acute insomnia is the inability to consistently sleep well for a period of less than a month.

3. Chronic insomnia lasts for longer than a month. It can be caused by another disorder, or it can be a primary disorder. Its effects can vary according to its causes. They might include being unable to sleep, muscular fatigue, hallucinations, and/or mental fatigue.

You have some time to read questions 16-20.

30 seconds pause

Now listen and answer questions 16-20.

A survey of 1.1 million residents in the United States conducted by the American Cancer Society found that those who reported sleeping about 7 hours per night had the lowest rates of mortality, whereas those who slept for fewer than 6 hours or more than 8 hours had higher mortality rates. Getting 8.5 or more hours of sleep per night increased the mortality rate by 15%. Severe insomnia-sleeping less than 3.5 hours in women and 4.5 hours in men-also led to a 15% increase in mortality. However, most of the increase in mortality from severe insomnia was discounted after controlling for comorbid disorders. After controlling for sleep duration and insomnia, use of sleeping pills was also found to be associated with an increased mortality rate.

The lowest mortality was seen in individuals who slept between six and a half and seven and a half hours per night. Even sleeping only 4.5 hours per night is associated with very little increase in mortality. Thus mild to moderate insomnia for most people is associated with increased longevity and severe insomnia is only associated with a very small effect on mortality.

As for treatment for insomnia, it is important to identify or rule out medical and psychological causes before deciding on the treatment for the insomnia. Attention to sleep hygiene is an important first line treatment strategy and should be tried before any pharmacological approach is considered.

That's the end of Section 2. You now have half a minute to check your answers.

30 Second pause

Now turn to Section 3.

SECTION 3

You are now going to listen to someone talking about the history of Oxford university. First you have some time to look at questions 21-25.

30 seconds pause

Now listen to the talk and answer questions 21-25.

Narrator: Good morning, ladies and gentlemen. Today we are very honored to have professor Lincoln, who is going to give us a talk about the history of Oxford University. Let's welcome.

Professor Lincoln: Thank you, good morning. As requested, first of all, I will give you a very brief introduction about the history of the Oxford University.

Oxford is a unique and historic institution. As the oldest English-speaking university in the world, it lays claim to eight centuries of continuous existence. There is no clear date of foundation, but teaching existed at Oxford in some form in 1096 and developed rapidly from 1167, when Henry II banned English students from attending the University of Paris.

In 1188, the historian, Gerald of Wales, gave a public reading to the assembled Oxford dons and in 1190 the arrival of Emo of Friesland, the first known overseas student, initiated the University's tradition of international scholarship. By 1201, the University was headed by a magister scolarum Oxonie, on whom the title of Chancellor was conferred in 1214, and in 1231 the masters were recognized as a university or corporation.

In the 13th century, rioting between students and townspeople hastened the establishment of primitive halls of residence. These were succeeded by the first of Oxford's colleges, which began as medieval "halls of residence" or endowed houses under the supervision of a Master. University, Balliol and Merton Colleges, established between 1249 and 1264, were the oldest.

Less than a century later, Oxford had achieved eminence above every other seat of learning, and won the praises of popes, kings and sages by virtue of its antiquity, curriculum, doctrine and privileges. In 1355, Edward III paid tribute to the University for its invaluable contribution to learning; he also commented on the services rendered to the state by distinguished Oxford graduates.

Oxford early on became a centre for lively controversy, with scholars involved in religious and political disputes. Husband Wyclif, a 14th-century Master of Balliol, campaigned for a bible in the vernacular, against the wishes of the papacy. In 1530, Henry VIII forced the University to accept his divorce from Catherine of Aragon. During the Reformation in the 16th century, the Anglican churchmen Cranmer, Latimer and Ridley were tried for heresy and burnt at the stake in Oxford. The University was Royalist in the Civil War, and Charles I held a counter-Parliament in Convocation House.

You have some time to look at questions 26-30.

30 second pause

Now listen and answer questions 26-30.

In the late 17th century, the Oxford philosopher Husband Locke, suspected of treason, was forced to flee the country. The 18th century, when Oxford was said to have forsaken port for politics, was also an era of scientific discovery and religious revival. Edmund Halley, Professor of Geometry, predicted the return of the comet that bears his name; Husband and Charles Wesley's prayer meetings laid the foundations of the Methodist Society.

The University assumed a leading role in the Victorian era, especially in religious controversy. From 1811 onwards the Oxford Movement sought to revitalize the Catholic aspects of the Anglican Church. One of its leaders, Husband Henry Newman, became a Roman Catholic in 1845 and was later made a Cardinal. In 1860 the new University Museum was the site of a famous debate between Thomas Huxley, the champion of evolution, and Bishop Wilberforce.

From 1878, academic halls were established for women, who became members of the University in 1920. Since 1974, all but one of Oxford's 39 colleges has changed their statutes to admit both men and women. St. Hilda's remains the only women's college.

In the years since the war, Oxford has added to its humanistic core a major new research capacity in the natural and applied sciences, including medicine. In so doing, it has enhanced and strengthened its traditional role as a focus for learning and a forum for intellectual debate.

That's the end of Section 3.

You now have half a minute to check your answers.

30 second pause

Now turn to Section 4.

SECTION 4

You are now going to listen to someone talking about amber. Listen to answer questions 31-40. First you have some time to look at questions 31-40.

45 second pause

Now listen to the talk and answer questions 31-40.

Good morning, everyone. Many people have been very interested in amber, which is a topic we have mentioned last week. Today, I'd like to tell you a thing or two about amber. First of all, how is amber formed?

Amber is a fossilized resin, although many people think it is tree sap. The formation of amber takes millions of years. Although a specific time interval has not been established for this process, the majority of amber is found within rocks that are approximately 30-90 million years old.

People have been studying the reasons why resin is produced? And there are many contrasting views, but it is mainly believed as a plant's protection mechanism. The resin may be produced to protect the tree from disease and injury inflicted by insects and fungi.

And amber can only be formed in very special condition. Recently some researchers complain that some ambers were found in the rocks undersea, and they think the process of amber formation is rather complex. One assumption is that because the amber's specific gravity is slightly over 1 and it floats in saltwater; therefore amber becomes concentrated in marine deposits, moved some distance from the original site. Trees and resin may be transported and deposited in quiet water sediments that formed the bottom of a lagoon or delta at the margin of a sea. Wood and resin are buried under the sediment and while the resin becomes amber, the wood becomes coal. Wet sediments of clay and sand preserve the resin well because they are devoid of oxygen.

Amber has been used for a long time; it is about 13,000 years ago. According to some studies, amber has been used for medical and ornament uses in ancient time, and today, it is even more widely used. For example, being combined with honey, it can be used to cure many disease, and it is used in the manufacture of smoking and alcohol, because of its flavor. Amber's place in culture and tradition has tourism value even, some museum even makes it an attraction.

Some ambers get great art value, but these ambers are rather rare. There is data here indicating the rarity of it. It says that there is only one among 100, no among 1,000 can be recognized as good ones.

Amber occurs in a range of different colors. As well as the usual yellow-orange-brown that is associated with the color "amber", amber itself can range from a whitish color through a pale lemon yellow, to brown and almost black. Other more uncommon colors include red amber, green amber, and even blue amber, which is rare and highly sought after.

Much of the most highly-prized amber is transparent, in contrast to the very common cloudy amber and opaque amber.

Ok, that is pretty much what I want to tell about amber today, if you are really interested, there are plenty of books about it in the library, you may go and have a look at some.

In the following, I would like to talk about…

That's the end of Section 4.

You now have half a minute to check your answers.

30 second pause

That's the end of the listening test.

You now have ten minutes to transfer your answers to the listening answer sheet.

第四周　星期三　Mobel Test 3

IELTS PRACTICE TEST

LISTENING

You will hear number of different recordings and you will have to answer questions on what you hear. There will be time for you to read the instructions and questions, and you will have a chance to check your work.

All the recordings will be played ONCE only. The test is in four sections At the end of the real test you will be given ten minutes to transfer your answers to an answer sheet.

Now turn to Section 1.

SECTION 1

You will hear a conversation between Scott and Vivian. First you have some time to look at questions 1-4.

30 secnd pause

Now listen to the conversation and answer the questions.

Scott: Vivian, you were not born in U. K. , weren't you?

Vivian: No, I was born in China.

Scott: Really? Which part of China? Do you grow up there as well?

Vivian: Beijing actually, I lived there till I was 15, but now we moved out.

Scott: Oh, I guess Beijing has changed a lot, you know the Olympic games?

Vivian: Yes, I have been back last year, and realized that it is a totally new place now, it is an international city now. I saw many foreigners in the street. What about you? Where did you grow up?

Scott: I grew up in England, in an area called Kent, near London.

Vivian: Has it changed much?

Scott: Umm … it has actually. I don't know if you've heard of the Channel Tunnel, linking England and France? It goes through Kent so they've built a big new railway and stations; it's a lot more built up.

Vivian: Yes, it is very famous. What did you normally do for fun when you were a child? Do you have brothers and sisters to play with?

Scott: I've got one brother; he's a year and a half younger than me so when we were growing up, we did everything together basically.

Vivian: Envy you. I am the only child at home.

Scott: Where I was brought up was a kind of village; it wasn't really a very rural area but it was the countryside and surrounding my house were trees and fields.

Vivian: Wow! That's lovely!

Scott: … and a football pitch, cricket pitch, all that kind of thing; I was always playing with my brother and friends … very easy to go and play sport and things like that.

You now have some time to look at questions 5-10.

45 seconds pause.

Now listen to the rest of conversation and answer questions 5-10.

Vivian: My cousin, my uncle's son, did quite the same thing; he played football with his friends quite a lot, but on the playgrounds. We do not have football pitches, things like that.

Scott: Yeah, what did you do, you liked gardening, many girls do?

Vivian: Not really, but my mother loved gardening.

Scott: I do too. Now I have a small area to place my plants. I really enjoy watering them.

Vivian: Good for you. And thinking back to your childhood. Do you have a lot of memories of your childhood? Or have you forgotten everything?

Scott: I have forgotten quite a lot, but I think that childhood during my days seemed to be more exciting than kids now.

Vivian: You know, when you talk to students, they're always playing computer games and watching films and this kind of thing. Presumably you didn't…well, like me, we didn't have computers. They would probably think it was very boring a few years ago, but you think it was more exciting.

Scott: I think so, yeah. I enjoyed being able to chase around with my friends and my brother enjoyed like, shooting the birds with a stone sometimes. But I think now, it's rather difficult to do so. And I think now, children tend to stay indoors quite a lot. I remember I used to ride a bike too in the park.

Vivian: You see, you don't see many children riding bikes now, do you?

Scott: No.

Vivian: I think actually, thinking of my memories, most of them are about outside life … jogging my memory, talking about this now, you know, in the park, in the countryside …

Scott: That's my ideal childhood, yeah.

Vivian: Very sort of free, just going out … and also, I don't think my parents worried about me going out with my brother, it seemed quite safe. Maybe they did worry, I don't know. I sense they didn't mind us going out, playing outside.

Scott: I think Chinese parents might be a little more nervous than European parents; my parents did warn us quite a lot not to go out and did limit the time we should be returning, but it was generally still very safe during my days and besides, there were not that many vehicles on the road.

Vivian: Yes, Beijing is very safe. It's a good place from that point of view, bringing up children; it's not too dangerous, there aren't many kidnappers and people like that around.

Scott: That's good, UK is quite safe as well, not as safe as Beijing though.

Vivian: But I love this place, very clean. People are friendly, you know.

Scott: Yeah, generally, it is a nice place to stay.

Vivian: Yes, good to talk to you, I think I need to go now.

Scott: Ok, talk to you next time. Bye.

Vivian: Bye.

That's the end of Section One.

You now have half a minute to check your answers.

30 second pause

Now turn to Section Two.

SECTION 2

You will hear a policeman giving a talk on the prevention of car theft.

First you have some time to read questions 11-20.

30 second pause

Now listen to the talk and answer questions 11-20.

Policeman: Good evening. I know many of you students are the proud owners of your first motor vehicle and this evening I want to talk to you about some of the things you can do to make sure your car or motorbike isn't stolen.

I'll start with a few facts and figures to put you in the picture. Car theft is a widespread problem. In this country alone one car is stolen every 32 seconds. That's almost a million cars each year. And of those, 40 per cent are never recovered. And don't think that just because your car might be a bit old and beaten-up looking no one will steal it. Any car can be stolen. Anywhere. Most thefts occur in residential areas, often from the front of the house or even from inside the garage. Some areas that are especially dangerous are shopping centers and parking lots, particularly at sports events. Most car thieves don't need to break into the car. They usually gain entry through unlocked doors and many times they find the key in the ignition. In fact, one in five stolen cars had the keys left in the car. Isn't that amazing? Twenty per cent of drivers left the keys in the ignition of an unlocked car! Who steals cars? Well, there are basically two kinds of car or bike thieves – joyriders aged about 15 to 21, and professionals. This last group usually needs less than one minute to break into a locked car and they often steal cars to use in other crimes such as robberies. You are much less likely to get your car back if it's stolen by a professional, and if it's stolen by a joyrider. chances are it'll be a wreck when you do get it back. Joyriders have a very high accident rate.

What can you do to make sure your car isn't stolen? Well, first and most obviously, lock the car when you leave it. That includes locking the boot or hatchback and making sure all the windows are closed. Even a tiny gap allows a thief to insert a wire to prise open the lock button. Of course, don't leave the keys hanging in the ignition. And don't conceal a spare key inside or outside the car-thieves know all the hiding places. If your car breaks down, lock up before you go for help. Even if you can't start the car, a thief may be able to. Now since dusk to mid-evening are the peak hours for car theft, make sure you park in a well-lit area, preferably where there are plenty of passers-by, say near a busy store or a restaurant. Avoid leaving your keys with a garage or parking-lot attendant, choose the place you park yourself. Keep your driver's license and registration in your wallet or purse, not in the glove compartment of your car. You should also have a record of your car's vital statistics both in your wallet and somewhere at home. This can help with recovery in case of theft. And finally, it's a good idea to install some kind of safety device. There is a range available-from alarm systems that set off a buzzer or siren if an attempt is made to tamper with the car in any way, to fuel shut-off systems and time-delay ignition systems. Displaying a warning sticker will also help deter would-be thieves. They don't want to waste time on trying to steal a protected car. So, help us put car thieves out of business by using common sense, always locking your car, installing anti-theft devices and cooperating with the police by reporting any attempt at theft.

That is the end of Section 2.

You now have half a minute to check your answers.

30 second pause

Now turn to section 3.

SECTION 3

You will hear two students, Rose and Joy, discussing about broadcasting.

First you have some time to look at questions 21-30.

30 second pause

Now listen to the talk and answer questions 21-30.

Rose: Hi, Joy. How is your presentation going? I heard that you are going to do something on radio thing?

Joy: Yes, it's on broadcasting.

Rose: That sounds interesting. What are you going to do exactly? Why do you want to do that?

Joy: Well, you know. Broadcasting is a major industry in most nations. It represents a critical national resource for communicating information and culture, popular entertainment, news, and educational programs can be transmitted directly into people's homes.

Rose: That's right, but different countries have their own broadcasting system, right? How do they differ from that of the other countries?

Joy: That's easy, you know, the electromagnetic spectrum allows for only a limited number of broadcast stations, virtually all nations regulate broadcasting within their borders. Many nations operate their own broadcasting systems through a ministry of communications.

Rose: I see, where do they get money from? Do they earn money by themselves, or the government provides them fund?

Joy: That depends, in some countries where it is believed that broadcasting should represent an independent voice, tax revenues support a public broadcasting authority that is independent of the government. Other countries simply license private broadcasters who make their profits by selling advertising time, or they permit a mixed system of commercial and publicly supported stations.

Rose: That sounds very complex, right?

Joy: Well, yes, but not really. take America for example. The U.S. has a mixed system. Most American stations are advertiser supported; about one in ten, however, is non-commercial, and its income is derived from listener or viewer contributions, corporate donations, and government funding.

Rose: Advertisers? Why do they do that? I don't think many people listen to radios anymore. I never listen to radio now. I watch TV instead.

Joy: Well, yes, again, in the U.S., 98 percent of the households have a television and almost 100 percent have a radio. In a typical week, nine out of ten citizens are exposed to radio and television, and in the average American home the television set is on about 7 hours each day, and the radio is on more than 2 hours a day.

Rose: Really, I did not know that, in that case, radio still has a lot of audience then.

Joy: Exactly, I did not realize that before. But when the president of the U.S., for example, delivers an address, between 60 and 80 million Americans are likely to be listening. Because of these audience figures, advertisers in the U.S. alone spend more than $24 billion per year to broadcast commercials.

Rose: Do you happen to know, who are the main advertisers?

Joy: Yes. Broadcast programming is dominated by popular entertainment, news, and occasional educational shows. So any products that are related to the audience would be an advertiser.

Rose: That is interesting to know, so the internet is not going to replace everything?

Joy: No, at least not at present. Many people still prefer the traditional means of getting information, like reading newspaper, listening to radio or watching TV.

Rose: Maybe, I should go to buy a radio, and have a try. I really want to know what is on now.

Joy: You should do, you would not be disappointed.

Rose: Yes, I will do. Good luck to your presentation. I think people would enjoy listening to you.

Joy: Thank you, I hope so.

That's the end of Section 3.

You now have half a minute to check your answers.

30 second pause

Now turn to Section 4.

SECTION 1

You are now going to hear someone introducing the history of East End of London. Listen to answer questions 31-40. First you have some time to look at questions 31-40.

45 second pause

Now listen to the talk and answer questions 31-40.

Good morning, everyone. Today I will briefly introduce the history of East End of London. Many people do not know where exactly is East End. Actually, even Londoners have different ideas of where the East End is, so let's start by being clear.

To the west, the border is the City of London, to the south the River Thames, to the east the

A102M motorway and the River Lea and to the north, Victoria Park and Hackney Road.

500 years ago, the East End was no more than green fields through which an old Roman road from Colchester to the City of London passed. The landscape would have been dominated by the old Roman wall and the Norman St. Tim's Cathedral, which was some 180 feet taller than the present one.

Another main "road" into London was the Thames, and, in 1520, London's reputedly oldest riverside pub opened to serve thirsty seamen. First known as the Devil's Tavern, now the Prospect of Whitby, it was a meeting place for sailors from all over the world for some four hundred years.

Inland from the docks and warehouses, in the 1600s, the unpleasant, smelly and dirty trades were being established. This happened on the east side of London because the dominant west winds kept the smells away from what was to become the rich, fashionable and aristocratic West End.

The Docks and City areas were severely bombed during the Second World War, destroying much of the old Victorian London. Ship containerisation caused the docks to close in 1969, causing very high unemployment. The notorious Kray twins, who controlled the East End underworld rather like feudal lords, ruling their "manor" are not forgotten by East Enders, as a new campaign is soon to be launched to free Reggie Kray from imprisonment.

The area has been revived since the 1980s with the emergence nearby of a new financial centre headed by the Canary Wharf development. Government plans to make Stratford an International Rail Terminus are still subject to finance, but success will increase the speed of change in East London.

That's the end of Section 4.

You now have half a minute to check your answers.

30 second pause

That's the end of the listening test.

You now have ten minutes to transfer your answers to the listening answer sheet.

第四周　星期四　Model Test 4

IELTS PRACTICE TEST

LISTENING

You will hear a number of different recordings and you will have to answer questions on what you hear. There will be time for you to read the instructions and questions, and you will have a chance to check your work.

All the recordings will be played ONCE only. The test is in four sections. At the end of the real test you will be given ten minutes to transfer your answers to an answer sheet.

Now turn to Section 1.

SECTION 1

You will hear a telephone conversation between a customer and two insurance assistants.

First you have some time to look at questions 1-5.

30 second pause

Now listen to the conversation and answer questions 1-5.

Assistant l: Global Insurance. Good morning. Can I help you?

Elisabeth: Oh, hello. I'm ringing to report an accident.

Assistant 1: A car accident?

Elisabeth: Yes.

Assistant 1: Just hold the line a moment please. I'm putting you through to our motor insurance department.

Assistant 2: Hello?

Elisabeth: Hello.

Assistant 2: I understand you want to report an accident?

Elisabeth: Yes. My car's been damaged-someone came out in front of me …

Assistant 2: Could I just check a few personal details before we go any further?

Assistant: Oh, yes, sorry.

Assistant 2: Your name, first of all.

Elisabeth: It's George Tomas.

Assistant 2: Is that T-H-O-M-A-S?

Elisabeth: No, there is no H.

Assistant 2: Oh, OK … And your date of birth please?

Elisabeth: It's the fifth of October, 1978.

Assistant 2: … And lastly, I just need to check your address.

Elisabeth: Oh, actually I moved house last month so the street name's different. It's 30 Kinston Street. I think you've got 11 Grand Avenue on your records?

Assistant 2: I have. So I'll just make a note of that … That's fine.

Elisabeth: That's great.

Assistant 2: Right, now … Can you give me the policy number please?

Elisabeth: Oh, yes. 673894.

Assistant 2: I am afraid it should start with letters …

Elisabeth: Oh, I see, it's W-H-78093.

Assistant 2: That's it. And now I want to ask you something about the accident. Is that OK?

Elisabeth: Yes, that's fine.

Assistant 2: First of all, when did it happen?

Elisabeth: It happened at about 2:00 o'clock in the morning. It's too early, so I didn't call.

Assistant 2: I see … that should be today, the 16th of July. Is that right?

Elisabeth: It is.

You now have some time to look at questions 6-10.

30 second pause

Now listen to the rest of the conversation and answer questions 6-10.

Assistant 2: And are you able to provide any supporting evidence? I mean witness statements, that kind of thing?

Elisabeth: Well, I don't know, but I did report to police, is that OK? They came and measured up and checked the marks on the road.

Assistant 2: Yes, that's OK. Do you have any hospital report? I mean, do you have any medical problems, or any injuries?

Elisabeth: Only minor ones. It was mainly the car that got damaged luckily.

Assistant 2: OK. But we do recommend that you have a checkup anyway. Within twenty-four hours if possible.

Elisabeth: Yes, OK. I'II make an appointment today.

Assistant 2: Fine. And now, can you tell me where the accident happened?

Elisabeth: It's in front of the flying over in the city center, I was about to drive on to the flying over…

That's the end of Section One.

You now have half a minute to check your answers.

30 Second pause

Now turn to Section Two.

SECTION 2

You are now going to listen to someone talking about preparing for a holiday.

First you have some time to look at questions 11-15.

30 second pause

Now listen to the talk and answer questions 11-15.

When it comes to booking your next holiday there is a lot to think about. Which country do you want to visit? What kind of holiday do you want to have? Do you want a relaxing beach holiday with nothing in particular to do-or is an active holiday more the kind of thing you are after?

Whatever fits the bill, you need to start looking for that type of holiday in the country of your choice before you do anything else. Matching up the holiday with the country can be as easy as finding the best beach available, or it might be harder-if you want to go to Greece for example, finding the best location to go mountain biking might take a bit of research if you want to book the best experience possible.

You also need to think about what type of accommodation you would like to stay in. If you are the type of person who likes to know that every need will be catered for without you having to worry then a hotel might be the best option. And if you are going on an active holiday then you might like to opt for a hotel that has a spa and a swimming pool on site to help you unwind as well!

You have some time to look at questions 16-20.

30 second pause

Now listen to the rest of the talk and answer questions 16-20.

Alternatively you may prefer to opt for something that is more traditional to the country you are visiting. For example, if you are visiting Goa you could stay in one of their beach huts on stilts for a really authentic experience. Be prepared for less of the mod cons though!

It can help to make a shortlist of the things you want to do and then find out what the best location for a holiday would be. You also need to think about the type of person you are when planning your ideal holiday. Some people will book a trip based on what their friends or family members tell them about a particular location, but you need to bear in mind that what they enjoy may be very different from what you would enjoy, and you could end up having a less than satisfactory holiday as a result.

While it's a good idea to visit your local travel agent to see what they have available in the way of brochures, the best way to find your ideal holiday is to look online as you can do some research into the possible destinations that make it onto your shortlist.

Of course it depends on the type of person you are as to what you will enjoy the most. If you want the height of luxury then go for all inclusive hotels to stay in. If you want to cook your own meals then a B&B would be more suitable.

In the end we all have our own ideas about what makes the ideal holiday; so long as you find out what yours are you'll have a great time.

That's the end of Section 2. You now have half a minute to check your answers.

30 Second pause

Now turn to Section 3.

SECTION 3

You are now going to listen to two people, Cathy and Bob talking about a project.

First you have some time to look at question 21-25.

30 second pause

Now listen to the talk and answer question 21-25

Cathy: Hi. Bob. How are you? I heard that you were sick last week.

Bob: I'm OK now.

Cathy: What was the problem? It was the fish in the canteen? Many people complained of that.

Bob: I don't know. At first I thought it was flu, but then I felt dizzy and my eyes started to go blurry…

Cathy: I'm so sorry…that sounds serious…

Bob: It's OK, actually. I went to the doctor and he diagnosed me with eye infection. He gave me some medicine, and I'm starting to feel much better.

Cathy: I'm glad to hear that. Well, I'm also glad you're in today because we have to work on a new project together.

Bob: Great, who else are in the same group?

Cathy: No, no one else. Mr. Speary puts us together because we live close.

Bob: That could be fun! What do we have to do?

Cathy: Well, the project is mainly library research, you know, checking reference books for information, but we have to prepare a survey, which we have to use with people we know.

Bob: Great, what's the topic?

Cathy: It's to do with shopping over the last decade. We have to find out the changes on customers behaviour.

Now look at question 26-30

30 second pause

Now listen to the rest talk and answer question 26-30.

Bob: OK…so, what shall we do first?

Cathy: I think the first thing to do is to check the list of references he gave me. I will check in the library, would you be willing to look up some Information online? Once we're done with the reference checks, we can write the questions together.

Bob: That's fine, I'll do the Internet research. Maybe you only focus on the first five years, then I focus on the second five years, because the internet always get the latest information.

Cathy: That's a great idea.

Bob: So…what sort of shopping are we looking at? food, or drink, or clothes shopping…?

Cathy: Well, I wanted to do these, but there is another group doing that, so we can do something about electrical goods.

Bob: OK. Well, then, but first of all, I'll have to catch up on the notes from last week. Can you help me or are you busy?

Cathy: I've made you a copy of my notes already, to save you time. Here you are!

Bob: Wow, thanks, Cathy, that's so thoughtful! Well, shall we go for lunch now, my treat today?

Cathy: Thank you, but I have to go to a meeting this afternoon. Maybe tonight, we can have dinner together?

Bob: No, I am sorry, I have an appointment. How about tomorrow?

Cathy: Sure, great.

Bob: OK, see you tomorrow.

That's the end of Section 3.

You now have half a minute to check your answers.

30 second pause

Now turn to Section 4.

SECTION 4

You are now going to listen to someone talking about higher education.

First you have some time to look at question 31-40.

45 second pause

Now listen to the talk and answer question 31-40.

Ladies and gentlemen. In the last seminar we talked about secondary education, so today, we are going to discuss something about higher education.

Before we move on. I would like to put forward three of my assumptions, afterwards, I would like you to discuss a little bit about them. Now my three assumptions:

First, higher education is distinctively different from other forms of education not only because of the level of intellectual difficulty associated with its curriculum, but also because that curriculum is concerned with not yet completely solved problems.

Second, higher education is of fundamental importance to the healthy functioning of a democratic society because it is fundamental to how society thinks about itself. The main aim of higher education is to enable society to make progress through an understanding of itself and its world, in short, to sustain a learning society.

Third, higher education-in the traditional sense of an academic community enquiring into problems for their own sake-is under challenge from a view, articulated by government, which sees it as existing chiefly to enable other societal purposes to be achieved. Whilst recent Ministerial speeches have certainly acknowledged the traditional role of universities, the main emphasis has been on what higher education can do for others: equipping the labour force with the key transferable skills needed for employment, meeting the demand for higher level skills, transferring technology and know-how to firms, generating economic development, creating social inclusion etc.

Now can you please talk with people around about these assumptions? I would be very glad to hear some of your ideas, especially those who disagree with me.

…

Ok, great, now before we share the opinions, I would like to tell you the five reasons why I have chosen this.

First, because it is a good illustration of my main theme.

Second, because it is the link between research, scholarship and teaching which sustains higher education's claim to distinctive, and distinctively better, treatment in terms of resourcing, if not prestige, than other sectors of education. If the link is broken or, still worse, not found to exist, then a large part of higher education's claimed superiority disappears.

Third, because unless there are benefits to teaching, there is no theoretical case for doing research in universities at all.

Fourth, because as a matter of fact, resources for research are very often found for teaching, which is of course not the same as saying that expenditure levels on research are optimal.

Last, because the alleged link is often the basis for statements about the superiority of some institutions or departments over others, claims which need to be verified if we are to accept the resource and value implications.

Great, now I would like to have some of your ideas.

…

That's the end of Section 4.

You now have half a minute to check your answers.

30 second pause

That's the end of the listening test.

You now have ten minutes to transfer your answers to the listening answer sheet.

第四周 星期五 Model Test 5

IELTS PRACTICE TEST

LISTENING

You will hear a number of different recordings and you will have to answer questions on what you hear. There will be time for you to read the instructions and questions, and you will have a chance to check your work.

All the recordings will be played ONCE only. The test is in four sections. At the end of the real test you will be given ten minutes to transfer your answers to an answer sheet.

Now turn to Section 1.

SECTION 1

You will hear a telephone conversation between a customer and an agent at a company which ships large boxes overseas.

First you have some time to look at questions 1-10.

30 second pause

Now listen to the conversation and answer questions 1-10.

A: Good morning, New Container Shipping Agents. Can I help you?

B: Oh, yes, I'm ringing to make enquiries about sending a large box, a container, back home to Japan from the Australia.

A: Yes, of course. What can I do for you?

B: I am wondering if you can find some quotations for me.

A: Sure, I would be very glad, but first of all, I need a few details from you.

B: OK.

A: May I know your name please?

B: It's Joy Armstrong.

A: Can you spell your surname, please?

B: Yes, it's A-R-M-S-T-R-O-N-G.

A: I see, it that Armstrong?

B: Yes.

A: Thank you, and you say that you will be sending the box to Japan?

B: That's right.

A: And where would you like the box picked up from?

B: From my home, if possible.

A: Yes, of course. I'll take down the address now.

B: It's 32 Westmill Street.

A: 32 Westmill Street, I have taken that down, but I am not sure where that is?

B: It's in the downtown of Sydney. Actually, there is a huge supermarket in that street.

A:Oh, yes, I know it. And the postcode?

B: It's WS89SC.

A: Right … and have you measured the box? I mean the size of it.

B: Yes, it's 2.5m long …

A: Right.

B: 1.75m wide …

A: OK.

B: And it's 1.5m high or deep.

A: Great. So I'll calculate the volume in a moment and get some quotes for that. But first can you tell me, you know, very generally, what will be in the box?

B: Yes, there's mostly books and clothes.

A: OK.

B: And there's some DVDs I have collected.

A: OK. That's no problem, but is there any liquid, I mean things like wine, perfume etc?

B: Yes, there are two bottles of perfume. It's gift for my family, is that OK?

A: I am afraid not, because we cannot guarantee it could be safe.

B: That's OK, I will take that out.

A: Great, thank you. Thank you for your understanding.

B: That's no problem, anything else?

A: OK and what is the total value, do you think, of the contents?

B: Well, the main costs are the DVDs and the books–they'll be about £2,500 but then the clothes are about another five hundred–so I'd put down £3,000.

A: Great, I will take that down, and someone will come and pick it up today, or tomorrow.

B: That's great, thank you.

A: You are welcome, goodbye.

B: Bye.

That's the end of Section One.

You now have half a minute to check your answers.

30 second pause

Now turn to Section Two.

SECTION 2

You are now going to listen to someone talk about jogging.

First you have some time to look at questions 11-15.

30 second pause

Now listen to the talk and answer questions 11-15.

Today, I would like to talk about some general tips for avoiding injury while enjoying the sport of jogging. Jogging is somewhat unique as a fitness method in that it combines some of the rigors and intensity of running and aerobics but at a much more manageable pace for the average person. The major benefits include increased functioning of the heart and lungs, strength and toning of other muscles — also with aesthetic results — and general endurance. For some, they may feel the secondary effects: increased joint mobility, weight loss, and reduction in stress.

First and foremost, it is generally recommended that you check with your healthcare provider as to your overall physical condition before beginning a semi- or high-intensity exercise program such as this, particularly if you have a medical history.

For those already following a regular exercise regimen, especially if it is aerobic in nature, getting started in a jogging program may be a relatively smooth adjustment. For those to whom physical fitness of this nature may be new, the initial start may be at a slower pace. For all, however, the guidelines below are key to remaining injury-free and maximising the health benefits.

You have some time to look at questions 16-20.

30 second pause

Now listen to the rest of the talk and answer questions 16-20.

First of all, Preparation.

A proper diet is the basis for any fitness program, and the higher intensity, the more influence it has. This essentially means a minimum of three meals per day, with a total intake that includes all basic food groups and meets the needs of your basic body functions and the increased activity.

Hydration is a critical issue much like diet—but it is also affected by temperature, as losses are greater when sweating. The average person requires about 6-8 cups per day of fluids, and jogging may increase this to 12 or more, depending on intensity, duration, and surrounding heat. It is important to keep in mind that such losses include not only water, but also electrolytes such as sodium, potassium, magnesium, and calcium, and these need to be replaced as well. Uncompensated losses can lead to cramping and even disturbances in heart function. Most sports drinks are designed around the principle of restoring fluid and electrolyte balance during exertion.

In addition, the Key equipment:

Clothing appropriate to the weather, layered for easy adjustment in cooler temperatures; absorbent is best, to allow perspiration to evaporate—one of the body's primary cooling mechanisms.

Quality running shoes—features to look for include not only general fit, but also cushioning, flexibility, stability, sole thickness, and arch support; some of these may be considered "frills" for day-to-day use, but the additional and repetitive stress of jogging makes these particularly critical. Common injuries due to poor footwear include blisters, shinsplints, sprains, and even fractures.

…

That's the end of Section 2. You now have half a minute to check your answers.

30 second pause

Now turn to Section 3.

SECTION 3

You are now going to listen to someone talking to his professor about some techniques to help him assess his progress in learning English, First you have some time to look at question 21-25.

30 second pause

Now listen to the talk and answer question 21-25.

Alex is talking to his professor about some techniques to help him assess his progress in learning English.

Alex: Professor, I am quite puzzled recently, and I do not know how my English learning is going on.

Professor: Yes, many students have that problem, Maybe you can try some self-assessment techniques.

Alex: Self-assessment techniques, what do you mean?

Professor: Well, let me take one of my students as an example.

Alex: Great, thank you.

Professor: Well, the first thing he did is writing learning dairies. Basically, he writes everything down in his diary. he writes what he does in class. Then he writes about his feelings: if he enjoys activities or finds them boring.

Alex: This part is difficult for me. I felt unable to write anything negative.

Professor: But nobody needs to read your diary, Alex. You can write anything.

Alex: Actually, I wrote something sometimes. A few days ago I had an awful reading class. It was hot. I was tired, the grammar was difficult. I wrote exactly what I thought in my diary.

Professor: And did you reflect on this?

Alex: Yes.

Now you have some time to look at question 26-30.

30 second pause

Now listen to the rest of the talk and answer question 26-30.

Professor: And?

Alex: The same thing happened a few times. I realised that it usually happened in the reading classes. One of my problems was "time". I felt rushed.

Professor: So what are your conclusions?

Alex: I spoke to the lecturer about it. He thought I needed to practise my reading skills to try to read faster. I don't read much at all. So I think he had a point.

Professor: Have you done anything about this?

Alex: I've started reading the newspaper every morning. I time myself and see how quickly I can get the information. It works.

Professor: Have you noticed a difference in class?

Alex: Yes, but I think I need more time to practice.

Professor: That's true, reading speed needs time to be improved. Last time, we have been talking about the "progress cards". Have you been using them?

Alex: Yes, they're great. I did one yesterday.

Professor: Good, tell me what you did.

Alex: Well, you know yesterday, I had a listening class. Before the class, I wrote on a card several statements like: "I can catch the main idea"; "I can catch almost every word"; "I can get the attitude of the speaker", things like that.

Professor: Sounds good, how did you do later with the card?

Alex: Well, I keep the card in the class, and I try to tick them when I think I can do them. I have ticked two yesterday, "I can catch the main idea"; "I can catch almost every word"; but I still cannot get the attitude of the speaker.

Professor: Sure, it's hard, you need to be patient, if you keep doing that you would feel fine. Good luck.

Alex: Well, thank you very much indeed for your time and suggestions.

Professor: No problem, good bye.

Alex: Bye.

That's the end of Section 3.

You now have half a minute to check your answers.

30 second pause

Now turn to Section 4.

SECTION 4

You are now going to hear someone giving a lecture about water.

First you have some time to look at question 31-40.

45 second pause

Now listen to the lecture and answer question 31-40.

Water is one of the basic human needs. However, global coverage figures from 2002 indicate that, of every 10 people: roughly 5 have a connection to a piped water supply at home; 3 make use of some other sort of improved water supply, such as a protected well or public standpipe; 2 are unserved; which means we are facing water stress.

There are many factors that contribute to the water stress. Firstly, the population growth.

In 2000, the world population was 6.2 billion. The UN estimates that by 2050 there will be an additional 3.5 billion people with most of the growth in developing countries that already suffer water stress.

Secondly, the expansion of business activity.

Business activity ranging from industrialization to services such as tourism and entertainment continues to expand rapidly. This expansion requires increased water services including both supply and sanitation, which can lead to more pressure on water resources and natural ecosystems.

Thirdly, the rapid urbanization.

The trend towards urbanization is accelerating. Small private wells and septic tanks that work well in low-density communities are not feasible within high-density urban areas. Urbanization requires significant investment in water infrastructure in order to deliver water to individuals and to process the concentrations of wastewater–both from individuals and from business.

In addition, the climate change.

Climate change could have significant impacts on water resources around the world because of the close connections between the climate and hydrological cycle. Rising temperatures will increase evaporation and lead to increases in precipitation, though there will be regional variations in rainfall. Overall, the global supply of freshwater will increase. Both droughts and floods may become more frequent in different regions at different times, and dramatic changes in snowfall and snowmelt are expected in mountainous areas. Higher temperatures will also affect water quality in ways that are not well understood. Possible impacts include increased eutrophication. Climate change could also mean an increase in demand for farm irrigation, garden sprinklers, and perhaps even swimming pools.

Finally, water pollution is one of the main causes of water stress. Many pollutants threaten water supplies, but the most widespread, especially in underdeveloped countries, is the discharge of raw sewage into natural waters; this method of sewage disposal is the most common method in underdeveloped countries, but also is prevalent in quasi-developed countries such as China, India and Iran. Sewage, sludge, garbage, and even toxic pollutants are all dumped into the water. Even if sewage is treated, problems still arise. Treated sewage forms sludge, which may be placed in landfills, spread out on land, incinerated or dumped at sea. In addition to sewage, nonpoint source pollution such as agricultural runoff is a significant source of pollution in some parts of the world, along with urban stormwater runoff and chemical wastes dumped by industries and governments.

That's the end of Section 4.

You now have half a minute to check your answers.

30 second pause

That's the end of the listening test.

You now have ten minutes to transfer your answers to the listening answer sheet.

第四周　星期六　Model Test 6

IELTS PRACTICE TEST

LISTENING

You will hear a number of different recordings and you will have to answer questions on what you hear. There will be time for you to read the instructions and questions, and you will have a chance to check your work.

All the recordings will be played ONCE only. The test is in four sections. At the end of the real test you will be given ten minutes to transfer your answers to an answer sheet.

Now turn to Section 1.

SECTION 1

You are now going to listen to someone hiring a car. First you have some time to look at questions 1-5.

30 second pause

Now listen to the conversation and answer questions 1-5.

Woman: International Transportation, may I help you?

Man: Yes, I would like to hire a car for the weekend.

W: Sure, I just need to take down a few detail. First may I know your name please?

M: My name is George Smith.

W: Yes, Mr. Smith, may I know your address?

M: It's 6 Devon Road, Oxford.

W: How do you spell that?

M: It's D-E-V-O-N.

W: Thank you, and what is your telephone number?

M: My office number is 634096, but my extension is 54.

W: Extension 54, I got it. And what kind of car are you thinking of hiring?

M: What kinds of car do you have?

W: We mainly have two kinds, Grade C and Grade D.

M: Is there any difference? I mean the facilities.

W: Well, yes. but both kinds provide music equipment, although Grade C does not have air conditioning.

M: That is OK, how about mileage?

W: Yes, we charge both according to the mileage and the time you keep the car.

M: I understand, I have hired cars before. But do I have to pay tax for using the car?

W: No, the company will take care of that.

M: That is great, oh yes, just one more thing, do you have first aid kit?

W: Yes, but only for Grade C.

M: I will hire that one then, we are thinking of going to the countryside for the weekend, just in case the car might have some problem. I can handle it myself.

You have some time to look at questions 6-10.

30 second pause

Now listen to the rest of the conversation and answer questions 6-10.

W: OK, no problem. When would you come for the car, please?

M: I think I will come and get the car on Friday.

W: Friday, OK.

M: And one more thing, if I take the car on Friday afternoon, when should I return the car?

W: Well, actually you can keep the car as long as you like, since we charge according to the time, but in your case, I would suggest you to return it before eight o'clock on Sunday night, and you only have to pay for two days.

M: That's very kind of you. Does that mean if I return it on Saturday, I only need to pay for one day?

W: Well, yes. You may also return on Monday morning, but you will have to pay for two and half days.

M: I see, I think I will return it on Monday, because we may come back very late on Sunday. By the way, how much do I have to pay, and can I have a discount?

W: Well, it's 100 pounds a day, and we only give discount to some special company staff, I mean the business partners.

M: Great, I work in Global Car Washing, which I think has a membership of your company.

W: That's right, in that case, you can have 20 percent discount.

M: That's great.

W: And we can also provide you with some basic tools, like road map, flash light and a camp tent, if you need.

M: That's great, I was thinking of buying one myself. OK, thank you so much.

W: You are welcome, have a nice weekend. Goodbye.

M: Thank you, good bye.

That's the end of Section One.

You now have half a minute to check your answers.

30 second pause

Now turn to Section Two.

SECTION 2

You are now going to listen to someone talking about shopping.

First you have some time to look at questions 11-15.

30 second pause

Now listen to the talk and answer questions 11-15.

Why do people shop? This question has been examined by psychologists and personal finance bloggers for years and the reasons are usually broken down into the old needs vs. wants dilemma. I think it goes much deeper than that.

We buy things we budget for and things we need–food, clothing, transportation, shelter, climate control, and sometimes we buy things to replace items we've worn out or outgrown. Sometimes we buy things we want and that's okay so long as our decision is made with an idea of where the money is coming from and it isn't from high interest debt. It's also a good idea to make sure the money you spend on wants doesn't jeopardize your ability to meet your future needs.

But many times, we shop for other reasons:

1. We shop because we're mildly depressed. It's called retail therapy and it's no joke. In some people, shopping causes an increase in dopamine which causes you to feel happy for a short time.

2. We shop because "we deserve it". After a hard day at work, or a long day at home with the kids, shopping is your personal reward for the stress and overwhelming circumstances you've been through.

3. We shop to feel more in control. That cash or plastic in your hand gives you control over

your circumstances and human beings love to be in control. There's nothing like a salesperson working to make you happy.

4. We shop to make a point. Closely related to No.3, you may shop to prove that no one can tell YOU what to do. Your wife, your husband, your parents, or even a blog can't control you.

5. We shop to escape. Going through the mall is your escape from reality and it feels great to blow off everyone and everything and just clear your mind while you decide between royal blue and teal blue.

You now have some time to look at questions 16-20.

30 second pause

Now listen to the rest of the talk and answer questions 16-20.

6. We shop to be someone else. You really believe that those new shoes or that new iPhone will make your life better. Those shoes make you feel glamorous and that iPhone makes you feel important and part of the "in" crowd. Hopefully, your acquaintances will be jealous.

7. We shop to socialize. Shopping is your "day out" with the girls but it isn't just for women. No, men shop too, just check out Bass Pro Shops for the guys comparing camouflage overalls or trolling motors. Shopping satisfies our urge to socialize.

8. We shop on impulse. You shop out of habit, stopping by the mall every day on the way home from work, or every Sunday afternoon as your way to relax.

9. We shop to fool ourselves. You claim to get so much exercise at the mall, that all the walking is doing your body some good.

10. We shop to build our ego.

You love the attention salespeople give you and the way they compliment your choices. When your teenager doesn't want anything to do with you, your spouse is wrapped up in a project, or layoffs are coming at work, those salespeople at the mall can really build your ego.

The first step to overcoming a bad shopping habit is to discover why you're doing it in the first place. See if any of these reasons reverberate with you and then take the necessary steps to overcome it and give your budget a break. Here's a hint–the one that made you mad could be the one you need to work on!

That's the end of Section 2. You now have half a minute to check your answers.

30 second pause

Now turn to Section 3.

SECTION 3

You are now going to listen to two students talking about a research on greenhouse effect.

First you have some time to look at questions 21-25.

30 second pause

Now listen to the conversation and answer questions 21-25.

Tom: Lisa, you mentioned that you are studying greenhouse effect recently. Could you explain in a few words what the Greenhouse Effect actually means?

Lisa: Well, in simple terms … the Sun heats the Earth's surface and the Earth radiates energy back out into space. Some of the radiation gets trapped in the atmosphere by greenhouse gases. This trapped radiation warms the atmosphere and some of it goes back down to the Earth, making it hotter than normal. This is the greenhouse effect.

Tom: So is carbon dioxide the problem?

Lisa: Yes … and other gases too. Methane … being released from paddy fields…. commercial oil and gas from landfills … vegetation left to rot without oxygen … These days there are more greenhouse gases than ever because of human activities and especially the burning of fossil fuels.

You now have some time to look at questions 26-30.

30 second pause

Now listen to the rest of the conversation and answer questions 26-30.

Tom: Well, can this problem be solved? Or can the scientists foresee them?

Lisa: Well, yes, for example, ice caps melting and sea levels rising mean that eventually cities like London, New York, Sydney and Tokyo will be submerged.

Tom: It seems incredible … the scientists might be very worried.

Lisa: Well, some scientists are optimistic. They believe that positive feedbacks from ice clouds and their water vapour could have an impact on global warming. Other scientists are more skeptical. They suspect that we have been wrong in our initial analyses of the situation and might need to go back to the drawing board!

Tom: So are you saying that some scientists don't believe in the Greenhouse Effect?

Lisa: No, I wouldn't go that far. In fact, without the Greenhouse Effect the planet would be frozen and no life forms would exist.

Tom: Is there anything that could protect us from global warming?

Lisa: Yes! Volcanoes!

Tom: Volcanoes? Are you kidding me?

Lisa: No, I am serious. When a volcano erupts it throws debris up into the stratosphere. This protects the Earth from solar energy by scattering the sunlight. Of course the best thing that we can do is to address the problem seriously on a world level. That's where the Kyoto Treaty enters the picture. If all of the governments in the world would commit themselves to making a real effort to work together on this issue, we might be able to slow down the process and work out a solution.

Tom: So …how worried do we need to be?

Lisa: That depends. First of all, global warming isn't going to affect all areas of the planet to the same degree. Things like the collapse of glaciers take hundreds of years so we are talking about a slow process here.

Tom: Slow enough for us to do something to prevent a catastrophe?

Lisa: Well … let's hope so!

Tom: Wow, you seem have done a lot of research, good luck with your study.

Lisa: Thank you, I enjoy it. I will keep doing it.

That's the end of Section 3.

You now have half a minute to check your answers.

30 second pause

Now turn to Section 4.

SECTION 4

You are now going to listen to someone talking about the history of cosmetics. First you have some time to look at questions 31-40.

45 second pause

Now listen to the talk and answer questions 31-40.

Good afternoon, everyone. In today's session, we will talk about cosmetics, especially the history of it.

Cosmetics, or "make-up", refers primarily to colored products intended to alter the user's appearance. Or more generally speaking, cosmetics are substances used to enhance the appearance or odor of the human body.

The manufacture of cosmetics is currently dominated by a small number of multinational corporations that originated in the early 20th century, but the first archaeological evidence of cosmetics usage was found in Egypt around 3500 BC during the Ancient Egypt times with some of the royalty having makeup. The Ancient Greeks and Romans also used cosmetics. The Romans and Ancient Egyptians used cosmetics containing poisonous mercury and often lead. The ancient kingdom of Israel was influenced by cosmetics as recorded in the Old Testament approximately 840 BC. The Biblical book of Esther describes various beauty treatments as well.

In the Middle Ages, although its use was frowned upon by Church leaders, many women still wore cosmetics. A popular fad for women during the Middle Ages was to have a pale-skinned complexion, which was achieved through either applying pastes of lead, chalk, or flour, or by bloodletting. Women would also put white lead pigment that was known as "ceruse" on their faces to appear to have pale skin.

Cosmetic use was frowned upon at many points in Western history. For example, in the 1800s, make-up was used primarily by prostitutes, and Queen Victoria publicly declared makeup improper, vulgar, and acceptable only for use by actors. Adolf Hitler told women that face painting was for clowns and not for the women of the master race.

Women in the 19th century liked to be thought of as fragile ladies. They compared themselves to delicate flowers and emphasised their delicacy and femininity. They aimed always to look pale and interesting. Paleness could be induced by drinking vinegar and avoiding fresh air. Sometimes ladies discreetly used a little rouge on the cheeks, and used "belladonna" to dilate their eyes to make their eyes stand out more. Make-up was frowned upon in general especially during the 1870s when social etiquette became more rigid.

By the middle of the 20th century, cosmetics were in widespread use by women in nearly all industrial societies around the world.

Cosmetics have been in use for thousands of years. The worldwide annual expenditures for cosmetics today is estimated at $19 billion. Of the major firms, the largest is L'Oréal, which was founded by Eugene Schueller in 1909 as the French Harmless Hair Colouring Company. The market was developed in the USA during the 1910s.

That's the end of Section 4.

You now have half a minute to check your answers.

30 second pause

That's the end of the listening test.

You now have ten minutes to transfer your answers to the listening answer sheet.

第四周　星期日　Model Test 7

IELTS PRACTICE TEST

LISTENING

You will hear a number of different recordings and you will have to answer questions on what you hear. There will be time for you to read the instructions and questions, and you will have a chance to check your work.

All the recordings will be played ONCE only. The test is in four sections. At the end of the real test you will be given ten minutes to transfer your answers to an answer sheet.

Now turn to Section 1.

SECTION 1

You are going to listen to someone calling the visa office about visa application.

First you have some time to look at questions 1-5.

30 second pause

Now listen to the conversation and answer questions 1-5.

Mr. Jenkins: Good morning, Britain Visa Office, how can I help you?

Student: Yes, I have several questions to ask concerning visa application.

Mr. Jenkins: Sure, go ahead.

Student: Yes, thank you. First of all, I am wondering if I can have more than one visa?

Mr. Jenkins: It is not possible to hold more than one visa or entry clearance. If your circumstances change you should always inform the Home Office before you leave the UK so that your permission to stay can be curtailed. Once your permission to stay has been curtailed you will be able to apply for a new visa overseas.

Student: Can my friend or family member in the UK apply for my visa for me?

Mr. Jenkins: Visas for the UK can be issued only at British Missions overseas. If you need a visa, you must get it before you travel to the UK.

Student: Can somebody else fill in my application form for me?

Mr. Jenkins: Yes, but you must sign the application form personally to show that the information given is true and accurate. Giving false or misleading information, or failing to give important relevant information on a visa application form, or to an entry clearance officer, will be reason for an application to be refused.

Student: Can I apply for a long-term visa?

Mr. Jenkins: You should give careful consideration before applying for a long-term visit visa valid for 1, 2, 5 or 10 years as there is the possibility that the visa may be refused, or issued for a shorter period than you have applied for. This could happen if the evidence you provide does not support a long term visit visa application or does not meet the entry clearance criteria. If the application is refused or the visa is issued for a shorter period, you will not be refunded your application fee. There is no automatic entitlement to a 1, 2, 5 or 10 year visit visa.

Before You hear the rest of conversation, you have some time to look at the questions 6-10.

30 second pause

Now listen to the rest of the conversation and answer questions 6-10.

Student: I was told that we may need to provide biometric information, but what is "biometric" information?

Mr. Jenkins: All UK visa applicants, save for those benefiting from a limited number of exemptions and exceptions, are required to provide biometric data as part of the application process, we take 10-digit finger scans and a digital photograph for our records.

You will have to go in person to your nearest visa application centre to provide your biometrics and submit your application.

Your visa application will not be processed until you have provided the necessary biometric information. The finger scans are electronic so staff do not need to use any ink, liquid or chemicals. You will have your digital photograph taken at the same time and the whole procedure should take no more than five minutes to complete. You should make sure that you do not have any decoration, or any cuts or other markings on your fingertips before having your finger scans. You should also make sure that if you have any cuts and bruises on your face, they have healed or disappeared before you have your photograph taken. Digital photographs must be of your full face and you should not wear sunglasses, a hat or any other head covering, unless you wear it for cultural or religious reasons but the face must not be covered.

Student: Why may I need to attend an interview?

Mr. Jenkins: When a visa officer cannot make an immediate decision about whether you qualify for a visa, you may be asked to attend an interview. We aim to do this within 15 working days from the date the visa officer assesses your application.

Student: Thank you so much, that's all very helpful.

Mr. Jenkins: You are welcome, good luck.

Student: Thank you.

That's the end of Section One.

You now have half a minute to check your answers.

30 second pause

Now turn to Section Two.

SECTION 2

You are now going to listen to someone talking about the benefits of using pensions to save for retirement.

First you have sometime time to look at questions 11-15.

30 second pause

Now listen to the talk and answer questions 11-15.

Good evening, listener. Today I am going to tell you a thing or two about the benefits of using pensions to save for retirement. First of all, what is a pension? A pension is designed to help you fund your retirement and replace the income you are no longer receiving from working. It can fit alongside all your other savings, from bank and building society accounts to property.

You could think of pensions as the first of three important ways to support your retirement. The second may be your home and the third, all your other savings and investments such as deposit accounts and shares. Your retirement income may come from any combination of the three.

There are three main categories of pension provision to consider: state pensions, company schemes and individual pensions.

There are several benefits of using pensions to save for retirement:

Firstly, tax relief. When you save in a pension the taxman helps to increase your pension pot by providing tax relief, subject to certain limits.

If you have an individual personal pension, your contributions have already been taxed before they go in to your fund. Any basic rate tax is then refunded back to your plan by the taxman. Higher rate taxpayers can claim back additional tax relief through a self-assessment tax form.

If you have a company pension tax relief works in a slightly different way. Contributions are deducted from your gross salary before income tax. As income tax is based on your pay after deducting your contributions you automatically receive tax relief at your highest rate.

Secondly, tax-efficient growth: Money in your pension fund grows largely free of tax. This can help to boost the amount you have in you fund. Remember that the value of your fund can go down as well as up and you may not get back your original investment.

Thirdly, employer contributions: With company pensions your employer makes contributions to your pension, increasing the amount going into your fund. Depending on the scheme they may at least match the contributions you make, or pay even more. To see how this can really help boost your pension pot-read more about company pensions.

Next, access to tax-free cash in retirement: When you take your benefits you may have the option of taking up to 25% of the pension fund you have built up as tax free cash. So if you build up a fund of £100,000, for example, you may be entitled to take £25,000 as a tax free lump sum.

Finally, access to investing in funds: By saving in a pension, you're able to put your money in a range of investments, such as the stock market, commercial property, bonds, and funds. The range of investments will depend on the scheme.

You may need more money than you think in retirement.

Average life expectancy is increasing, meaning that the length of your retirement could last longer than you expect. So it's important to think about the income you're likely to need for your retirement and the ways in which you can generate it.

Saving in a pension is a tax-efficient way of building an income and should ideally form part of your overall retirement plan.

That's the end of Section 2. You now have half a minute to check your answers.

30 second pause

Now turn to Section 3.

SECTION 2

You are now going to listen to some students asking a professor some questions about degree application.

First you have some time to look at questions 21-25.

30 second pause

Now listen to the discussion and answer questions 21-25.

Narrator: Good morning, everyone. Today we are very lucky to have Professor Adams, who is going to give us an insight into the undergraduate degree application. Let's welcome Professor Adams.

Adams: Thank you, good morning. I am very glad to be here with you all to talk about the undergraduate degree application. I would suggest us to take a question and answer approach. I mean, you ask me questions; I answer them, so that we can make this more relative. Does anybody have a question now?

Student 1: Yes, Professor Adams. I would like to know who can use the undergraduate degree application?

Adams: Yes, basically, all the Undergraduates who have completed 90 credits or are earning an undergraduate certificate may use the undergraduate degree application.

Student 2: I think I'm eligible to use this application but I can't get into the system. What should I do?

Adams: Check your total number of credits or make sure that paperwork for your certificate program has been processed. If you meet the requirements, please inform your college office that you are having problems.

Student 1: What if I don't see the graduation term I want?

Adams: The undergraduate degree application allows students to apply for graduation up to one year ahead of their expected graduation date. If you don't see the term in which you want to graduate, the deadline may have passed or you may be applying too early. If you believe your desired graduation term should be listed but it is not, or if you don't know which term to select, please contact your college office.

Student 2: I missed the deadline to apply; what should I do?

Adams: If possible, select a future term. Even though you may have missed the deadline for your desired term, you can still use the undergraduate degree application to apply for a future term. If you have extenuating circumstances and must graduate in a term not listed, please contact your college office.

Student 3: What happens if I cancel and exit before my application is completed?

Adams: If you choose to "cancel and exit" anytime during your application, you will lose all of the information you had previously entered. This means you will have to start at the beginning the next time you want to complete an application.

Before you hear the rest of the conversation, you have some time to look at questions 26-30.

30 second pause

Now listen to the rest of the conversation and answer questions 26-30.

Student 2: What if I have more than one degree to apply for in the same term?

Adams: If you have two degrees in the same college you will be able to apply for both degrees in one application. If you have two degrees in separate colleges, you will need to complete a separate application for each degree. You will have an opportunity at the end of your first application to return to the beginning of the undergraduate degree application and complete a second application.

Student 3: Can I go backward in my application if I think I entered something incorrectly?

Adams: You have the opportunity in the undergraduate degree application to return to a previous step to make changes. You will also be asked to review your application before you submit it; changes can be made at that time.

Student 1: I want my diploma sent to a third party; how do I do this?

Adams: To send your diploma to a third party, enter the address in the "Diploma Address" field. Be sure to include "In care of" followed by the name of the person who will receive your diploma on the first line of the address field.

Student 3: How will I know if my application has been successfully submitted?

Adams: Once you hit "submit" at the end of the application, you will see a screen confirming the successful submission of your application. You will also be asked to print a copy for your records.

That's the end of Section 3.

You now have half a minute to check your answers.

30 second pause

Now turn to Section 4.

SECTION 3

You are going to hear someone introducing a coming lecture.

First you have some time to look at questions 31-40.

45 second pause

Now listen to the introduction and answer questions 31-40.

Professor Smith has spent the past 15 years examining water policy and its implications for resource management. He has written and edited three books and published over 60 scholarly journal papers in this area. His work has covered the difficult public policy dilemmas associated with water allocation in Australia and India.

Professor Smith has been the Executive Director of this university since 2007. His recent appointment as Professor of Applied Economics reflects the University's commitment to regionally-relevant research.

The lecture is the second of three lectures in the University's Climate, Sustainability and Society lecture series. In the series, prominent speakers will draw on science, social science and economic perspectives to address the issues surrounding climate change and sustainability.

The Climate, Sustainability and Society lectures form an integral part of the Climate, Sustainability and Society cross-disciplinary, cross-campus subject that is offered for the first time this semester at different campuses of this University.

The first lecture by the leading scientist and climate change authority, Professor Barrie Bush, proved highly popular with around 330 people in attendance at the Lecture Theatre and 120 tuning in by video-conference.

Members of the public are invited to join staff and students for the second and third sessions in this innovative lecture series. The second lecture commences at 6:30 pm in the Lecture Theatre on Wednesday 26 August.

The third and final lecture of the series by public ethics/applied philosophy expert, Professor Clive Hamilton, is at 6:30p.m. on Wednesday 23 September.

First of all, I would like to give you some background information.

Climate, Sustainability and Society is a cross-disciplinary, cross-campus subject that is being offered for the first time in Semester 2, 2009. This first-year level subject introduces students to economic, scientific and sociological approaches to sustainability in the context of climate change.

It has been developed by the Faculties of Law and Management, Science, Technology and Engineering and Humanities and Social Science. It is planned for future offerings of the subject to occur across four or more campuses.

The teaching will take a problem-based approach through which students will develop a recognition and knowledge of the causes and impacts of climate change and the potential scientific, social and economic responses.

It is anticipated that students who successfully complete the subject will demonstrate an awareness of the theoretical and practical tools available to bring advanced decision making to environmental management.

An integral part of this subject is a series of public lectures presented by leading thinkers who represent a range of approaches to issues of sustainability and climate change in different contexts.

Along with members of the public, students who are enrolled in the subject will attend these lectures to experience the nature and shaping of public debate and to gain an appreciation of the relationship between advocacy and enquiry.

The students will be guided in their listening and note taking through the provision of four or five key questions provided prior to the public lecture. Their response to the questions will form part of subsequent class discussion.

These lectures will be video-conferenced between venues and filmed to allow students access to the content after the lectures. In subsequent years, these films may also be shown to later cohorts of students as a stimulus to debate and discussion.

That's the end of Section 4.

You now have half a minute to check your answers.

30 second pause

That's the end of the listening test.

You now have ten minutes to transfer your answers to the listening answer sheet.